ENGLISH COUNTRYSIDE
EMBROIDERY

By the Same Author:

The Compleat Strawberry
English Garden Embroidery

ENGLISH COUNTRYSIDE EMBROIDERY

A Treasury of Over 50 Original Needlepoint Designs

STAFFORD WHITEAKER

BRACKEN BOOKS
LONDON

FOR GRAHAM CROFT NICHOLSON

Copyright © Stafford Whiteaker 1988
Still Life Photography © Century Hutchinson 1988

Originally published by Century Editions, an imprint
of the Random Century Group Ltd,
20 Vauxhall Bridge Road,
London SW1V 2SA

This edition published 1992 by Cresset Press and
distributed by Bracken Books, an imprint of Studio
Editions Limited, Princess House, 50 Eastcastle Street,
London W1N 7AP, England

ISBN 1 85170 973 8

Designed by Clare Clements
Photography and styling by Sue Atkinson
Embroidery executed by The Ladies' Work Society,
the Benedictines of Turvey and the author
Photograph of the author by Martin Poole
Charts by Colin Salmon
Stitch illustrations by Colin Salmon and Anthony Duke

Set in Linotron ITC Cheltenham
by SX Composing Ltd, Rayleigh, Essex

Printed and bound in Italy
by New Interlitho S.p.a., Milan

CONTENTS

INTRODUCTION

From upland hills, snowy mountains, great woods, pastures for sheep and cattle, long lanes bordered with hedgerows to flower-filled cottage gardens, the English countryside epitomizes that dream of peace and natural beauty that most of us desire.

English style, familiar but not coarse, and elegant but not ostentatious.
Samuel Johnson, 1709-1784

For centuries this countryside has been the inspiration for the themes and motifs of the embroiderer, and just an hour on a field footpath will show how this remains true today. I have found patterns in my cottage garden, in walks down my lane through the seasons of the year, and by wandering along the river and through the fields of my farming neighbour. The Victorians enjoyed the pursuits of the countryside and I have included designs based on motifs found in Victorian embroidery styles and in country churches – those steeples and towers floating over the English landscape.

In the end, whoever loves the flowers, fields, hedgerows, wild creatures, sunlight and shadow, tree and wood of the countryside, whoever reaches thankfully for a wild strawberry or stands in silent awe before the slow rising of the grey wings of a heron from the river, must love this world. What we embroider is always from the world around us so let the small works of our hands be in praise of it.

HOW THE BOOK IS ORGANIZED
The purpose of this book is to provide entertainment and pleasure not only in working the patterns in needlepoint, but also in reading about the countryside and embroidery and in exercising your own creativity in deciding what to do, choosing colours, and 'mixing and matching' motifs from more than one pattern.

Detailed needlework instructions can be intimidating even to experienced embroiderers, and there are plenty of craft manuals devoted to technique, so I have tried in the sections 'The Art of Needlepoint' and 'Stitch Techniques' to pro-

The bloom on ripe cherries and children's cheeks reminds us of the goodness of life, and the perfect setting is the countryside.

vide some basic stitching instruction, a few new stitch ideas, and straightforward tips on doing the work. This is a pattern book based on a centuries-old tradition and while each pattern gives suggested colourways, I hope you will choose those that most please you.

TERMINOLOGY
Many people seem confused about the 'right' name for needlepoint. Is it needlepoint, canvaswork, or tapestry? 'Tapestry' is always incorrect for it means a *woven* work. The term embroidery is a general one, and, in England, 'canvaswork embroidery' is deemed correct when expert embroiderers are talking among themselves about embroidery on soft or hard canvas. However, in this book, I most frequently use 'needlepoint' as this is now the popular term and the one most widely in common use.

THE CREATIVE SPIRIT
Mankind seems always to have liked decoration, whether on the walls of caves, paint on the face, a fine dress, or the embellishment of plain cloth with stitches. The methods and styles explored to give expression to this artistic compulsion are legion and have little bearing on culture or age. Embroidery is just one manifestation of this creative spirit, so our impulse to do it is a deep-felt response to both our inner feelings and the world around us. All artistic creativity seems a combination of this awareness of our senses with a compulsion to express our individuality. What we create is, thus, uniquely our own. Even when two skilled embroiderers set out to do the same pattern, there will be subtle differences in the end result.

Behind every response to these feelings is an artistic heritage that sets us firmly within our culture and times so that our efforts become one more contribution to this inheritance. From the exquisite work of the unknown craftsmen who laid the mosaic floor of a Roman villa in Colchester to the tapestry designed by Graham Sutherland for the new Coventry Cathedral, England abounds with over a thousand years of such artistic heritage. Surrounded as we are by such cultural wealth, we take much of it for granted, often not stopping to reflect on how much it adds to the pleasure of ordinary life nor how much it influences the way we see our country and ourselves. Just as in Elizabethan days when an embroiderer drew upon the past inheritance of ancient herbals to portray plants in silk and wool, so contemporary English decorative art and domestic styles continue to draw inspiration from the past. Among the most influential of these – and perhaps the most beautiful of all since it is a living work of art – is the English landscape.

No lovelier hills than thine have laid
  My tired thoughts to rest:
No peace of lovelier valleys made
  Like peace within my breast.

Thine are the woods whereto my soul,
  Out of the noontide beam,
Flees for a refuge green and cool
  And tranquil as a dream.

My breaking seas like trumpets peal;
  Thy clouds – how oft have I
Watched their bright towers of silence steal
  Into infinity!

My heart within me faints to roam
  In thought even far from thee:
Thine be the grave whereto I came,
  And thine my darkness be.
        'England', Walter de la Mare, 1873-1956

COUNTRY LIFE
Wandering through cottage gardens filled with flowers and down endless lanes deep in boughs of leaves and blossom, it is easy to understand why the English love their countryside. Almost everyone dreams of living in a cottage at the end of a lane where roses ramble over the fence and the garden path is edged with sweet pinks, red poppies, fragrant iris and swaying hollyhocks. This idyllic scene is the image that the English hold dear and the one that visitors take back home.

There'll always be an England
While there's a country lane,
Wherever there's a cottage small
Beside a field of grain.
        'Song, 1939', Hughie Charles

Even today when most people must work in cities, they save towards a weekend retreat in the country. It is a small place, maybe thatched, nestled in a fold between field and hedge and bound with entwining roses and honeysuckle. In front, like an apron of many colours, is one of nature's and man's most successful achievements – the cottage garden.

This longing for the countryside and the romantic idea that it is always filled with flowers, butterflies, and the pursuits of gentle living and good food, is not a modern one. Love of the country lies deep in the English character. Here is an 1891 description of a desirable country cottage:

A pebbled pathway edged by mossy stones leads up to it through beds of roses and petunias, nasturtiums and phloxes, interspersed with currant-bushes and raspberry canes. Its red-tiled roof and crumbling chimney stack stand picturesquely out against a background of plum and walnut, apple and pear trees, and its latticed windows peep cosily out of a cluster of vines.

We are so accustomed to seeing or having a garden near our homes, no matter how small, that it seems unimaginable that these did not always exist. Until people left fortified castles and small communities where there was little space for growing plants, there were few individual gardens as we know them. Oddly enough, it was the great plague of 1349 that provided the catalyst for change. The countrywide infection decimated the population and began to break up the feudal communities where land was rented at a premium by the peasant. In those terrible years one-third of the population of England perished and, subsequently, labour was scarce. Peasants demanded high wages and got them. They also got the lands vacated by those who had died. Gradually homesteads arose and with them came small plots of land.

In those days, flowers were mostly grown for their use in flavouring foods. These earliest gardens, with a few fruit trees, herbs, vegetables

Cows still stand in the Red Lake River near my home as in this painting: The path by the water lane.

and crowded groups of self-seeded flowers, set the original pattern for the cottage garden which has lasted until today. Where an old cottage has not been 'done up' and modernized with flower beds, paths and pretty but rather exotic flowering trees, that original cottage garden design persists. The small orchard of apples, pears, plums and cherries, the patch for cabbages and the long rectangle for other vegetables can still be seen. Around such an unspoiled cottage a rusted wire arbour holds a tangled rose, pansies still lift up saucy faces here and there, the path has long since become overgrown with 'johnnie jump-ups' and weeds, ivy holds old bricks together, and walls still support pink roses, honeysuckle and blackberry. A tangled mass of rose catches at your clothes and forbids you to go further. There is a rush of wings and a panic cry from a bird as you pull open the door and disturb its nest above in the eaves. Inside, the air is chilled even in high summer, the hearth empty and black, the quarry-tiled floor shattered where some passing winter visitor has chopped kindling for his fire, and even the sunlight of a summer afternoon hardly enters through the broken panes of glass in the small windows. In spite of all this, you immediately want to set about bringing the place back into domestic use – the dream has possessed you.

Come live with me and be my love,
And we will all the pleasures prove,
That hills and valleys, dales and fields,
And all the craggy mountains yields.

There we will sit upon the rocks,
And see the shepherds feed their flocks,
By shallow rivers to whose falls
Melodious birds sing madrigals.

And I will make thee beds of roses
With a thousand fragrant posies,
A cap of flowers, and a kirtle
Embroidered all with leaves of myrtle;

A gown made of the finest wool
Which from our pretty lambs we pull;
Fair lined slippers for the cold,
With buckles of the purest gold.
'The Passionate Shepherd to His Love',
Christopher Marlowe, 1564-1593

There is just such a ruined cottage at the beginning of my lane. It hides behind a row of ugly evergreens – the kind that modern gardeners plant as a screen. Here the trees are massive, dark sentinels on guard. You must push your way through their thick arms to enter the garden. Even then, briar roses try to stop you. Scattered in a sea of weeds and wild grass, some hollyhocks, golden rod, a single lupin and the faded leaves of some iris greet you. Only an owl lives in the ruined cottage now and I hope it will be a long time before someone comes to 'do it up', for it is romantic, familiar, and at peace with its age and place.

A VICTORIAN INHERITANCE

Leisure among the new middle class of nineteenth century England was a rule of life as was the tireless pursuit of pleasure. For this privileged society, England offered a rich variety of entertainment including that of the countryside – there was hunting, shooting, fishing, racing, dazzling house parties, boating and bicycling, tennis, cricket and croquet, and all the restful pastimes of good gossip, books and needlework.

So comfortable were the upper- and middle-class Victorians that they could afford to patronize the arts. Painting and poetry flourished and most artists could live, unlike today, by their works alone. Music and literature were serious matters and artistic movements exciting and welcomed. The last thirty years of the nineteenth century burst with new ideas, new prophets and new artistic ardour.

Literal realism, brilliant colour and rich tone were the principal qualities of Victorian taste in art. Watercolour painting was a greatly preferred medium to which the well-bred, and those aspiring to be, could all turn their hand for better or worse. Queen Victoria had considerable talent and her portraits of her children are accomplished. Amateur artists painted and drew all aspects of contemporary life and imagination. In this way the landscape, countryside, architecture and people were all recorded. Fortunately, watercolours of favourite rooms were also

Corsets and stays may be out of fashion, but Victorian ladies remained elegant even adrift in a punt.

F. Percy Wild

A quiet spot for reading and apples gathered by the kitchen door are peaceful and visual delights of the countryside. No doubt the dog in the painting barked, but that is life too.

common so we can see where and how needlework was used in furnishing. The style and colour schemes may not always be to our contemporary taste but are excellent references for researching the authenticity of Victorian style. Since we admire Victorian furnishings, it is useful to know what kind of needlepoint patterns would have been favoured in the covering of a chair, stool or cushion.

SUMMER DAWN

Among the many artistic movements that captured the enthusiasm of the Victorians, there worked the solitary genius of William Morris (1834-1896). Poet, painter, author, designer, craftsman and a founder of modern socialism, his talent and industry were remarkable. He was the Renaissance man of the late Victorian era and his influence on arts and crafts, including embroidery, probably more than that of any other Victorian, fostered our twentieth century English concept of the place of man within the scheme of nature, and our contemporary belief in the relevance of the arts and crafts of the countryside to everyday life. He felt that the embroidery of his day, with the hard colours of aniline dyes, strove to reproduce nature rather than decorate fabric. He, therefore, condemned it and believed that civilization since the Middle Ages had been set on a wrong course. His embroidery and fabrics reflected medieval designs and an attempt to unite art and craft. Morris' aspirations and achievements to apply art to the objects of ordinary life helped create the Arts and Crafts Movement and influenced both his contemporaries and designers of future generations. The medieval achievements Morris so admired remain a foundation stone of English artistic work, including that of embroidery where the peerless poetry of Chaucer is matched by the ecclesiastical embroidery of unknown hands.

THE MEDIEVAL TREASURY

From 400 to 1400 AD Christianity in England was the fountainhead of inspiration for artistic achievements in all forms, as well as the motivating force behind a magnificent architectural epoch that created monasteries and churches whose very ruins today inspire silent awe and admiration. The English Romanesque period of art between William the Conqueror in 1066 and the twelfth century formed the background to the greatest period in English embroidery, known as *Opus Anglicanum,* which some would claim remains the greatest artistic achievement of this nation. It was at its peak during the thirteenth and fourteenth centuries and was in demand for ecclesiastical vestments and decorations all over Western Europe.

The subjects the embroiderers of those distant centuries took for their designs were almost always related to Christianity – the Holy Family, the Apostles, saints of the early church, Adam and Eve, demons and angels. When you consider

Plums, violets and, overleaf, hay-making are earth's gifts in a countryside of continual harvest and renewal.

H.J.Johnstone

Daydreaming makes one forget that chickens peck cabbages and put holes in turnips – but time slips by easily in a vegetable patch when peace abounds.

all the different kinds of angels, it is not surprising that medieval monks are said to have argued as to the *exact* number. There were 'appearing angels' who, according to scripture, have appeared quite often to mortal man – the most famous of which is Gabriel. Then there are 'accompanying angels' like Raphael who helped Tobias and his wife Sarah over many troubles. The 'mighty angels' are big indeed: the one in the Book of Revelation was 'wrapped in cloud, with the rainbow round his head; his face shone like the sun and his legs were like pillars of fire. His right foot he planted on the sea, and his left on the land. Then he gave a great shout, like the roar of a lion . . .' The angels we all hope will come to stay are the 'guardian angels', who watch over us.

The Archangels are the highest category: Uriel who rules the world; Raphael who rules the spirits of men; Raguel who takes vengeance; Michael who is set over the best part of mankind; Saraquael who rules over spirits; Gabriel, ruler of paradise, serpents and the Cherubim; Remiel whom God set over those who rise; Phanuel who rules those who repent and are given eternal life; and finally the angel whom no one wishes for – the fallen one, Lucifer.

BERLIN ARTWORK PATTERNS

While the Victorians admired medieval embroidery and later efforts, and the artistic outpouring of designs from William Morris and others, doing embroidery was one of the main indoor pursuits of gentlewomen and the majority of them continued to do needlepoint based on Berlin Artwork Patterns.

The popularity of Berlin Artwork patterns was to affect needlepoint design throughout much of Europe and America for many years, beginning in 1804 when a seller of prints in Berlin issued a coloured needlework design on squared paper. While black and white patterns on grid paper had been available for centuries, these designs were *coloured*. Anyone using them could not only copy the design square by square but also the colours chosen for the pattern.

These new coloured designs became extremely popular and another Berlin printer and bookseller named Wittich was encouraged by his wife to extend his business by making multiple copies of such patterns. Other publishers joined in. Between 1810 and 1840, a period of only thirty years, no less than 14,000 different copperplate designs of this kind were produced for needlework.

It was at this time that aniline dyes were invented. These chemical dyes, which produce very bright, often garish colours, were produced in Gotha in Germany and the yarns dyed with them were sold in Berlin. This gave a name to the style of embroidery and, thus, it became known as Berlin Woolwork or Berlin Work and the patterns as Berlin Artwork.

Loveliest of trees, the cherry now
Is hung with bloom along the bough,
And stands about the woodland ride
Wearing white for Eastertide.

Now, of my threescore years and ten,
Twenty will not come again,
And take from seventy springs a score,
It only leaves me fifty more.

And since to look at things in bloom
Fifty springs are little room,
About the woodlands I will go
To see the cherry hung with snow.'
'Loveliest of Trees, the Cherry now',
A. E. Housman, 1859-1936

This popularity of working from a pattern whether charted as in this book or printed directly on the canvas has not abated. Subject matter seems to have changed little with flowers still being the front-runner, although choice of wool colour changes with each passing interior-decorating fashion.

BEYOND THE GATE

In England, wild flowers and beautiful places are just a step outside the garden gate. What could be more inspiring than a walk down the long lanes of the English countryside where wild flowers, berries, dog roses and honeysuckle mingle together? Inspirations for embroidery abound with each season – primroses and hawthorn in spring, foxglove and elderflowers in summer, berries and gold leaves in autumn, and red and green holly as Christmas draws near.

From nearby fields come patterns of barley and oats, the wide oceans of wheat, orchard blossoms turned into the fruits of summer – apples, plums, quinces and cherries. The more we walk these lanes and fields, the more we will draw close to an awareness of the indispensable relationship of man and nature. As we embroider a flower or leaf and bring the countryside into our homes and hearts, so hopefully we will respond to this heritage with real efforts to nurture and care for it.

Sweet our strawberries and, overleaf, sweeter our dreams when the rivers of England flow gently in summer with willows green on greener banks, all silent as trout beneath clear water.

COUNTRY LORE

Many needlepoint projects are destined to be gifts, so adding the recipient's initials or name makes it very personal. Since needlepoint should last for many years, please also put in your initials and the date of the work. Future family, textile scholars and the merely curious will all appreciate knowing when it was done.

An old folk saying can be a charming conceit to add to a needlepoint. Here are a few from the countryside.

THE WEATHER

A cloudy morning bodes a fair afternoon.
Frost and fraud both end in foul.
Hail brings frost in its tail.
Make hay while the sun shines.
Mist in March, frost in May.
Rain before seven, fine before eleven.
Snow is the poor farmer's muck.
Two full moons mean a wet month.

DAYS OF THE WEEK

Monday's child is fair of face.
Tuesday's child is full of grace.
Wednesday's child is full of woe,
Thursday's child has far to go.
Friday's child is loving and giving.
Saturday's child works hard for his living.
The child that is born on the Sabbath day,
Is fair and wise, good and gay.

WOOD FOR BURNING

Beechwood fires burn bright and clear
If the logs are kept a year;
Chestnut's only good they say
If for years 'tis stored away;
Birch and firwood burn too fast,
Blaze too bright and do not last;
But ashwood green and ashwood brown
Are fit for a Queen with a golden crown.

COLLECTIVE NOUNS OF BIRDS

In the countryside birds rarely come in single numbers. Even city dwellers know that a group of cattle are a 'herd' or sheep a 'flock' but birds are a different matter.
Chickens: peep or brood
Crows: murder

Curlews: herd
Doves: flight
Ducks: team (in flight); paddling (on the water)
Eagles: convocation
Finches: charm
Geese: gaggle
Goldfinches: charm or trembling
Grouse: covey (single family); pack (larger gathering)
Gulls: colony
Hens: brood
Herons: siege
Jays: band
Lapwings: deceit
Larks: exaltation
Magpies: tiding
Mallard: flush
Nightingales: watch
Partridges: covey (family); brace (two)
Pheasants: nye (family); brace (two)
Pigeons: flight
Plovers: congregation
Quail: bevy
Ravens: unkindness
Rooks: clamour
Snipe: walk
Sparrows: host
Starlings: chattering
Swallows: flight
Swans: team
Swifts: flock
Teal: spring
Thrushes: mutation
Turkeys: rafter
Woodcock: fall
Woodpeckers: descent
Wrens: herd

THE ART OF NEEDLEPOINT

The terms 'art' and 'craft' are loaded with meaning, but they describe what millions of people do every day to express their creative impulse. In the art of needlepoint we are decorating even-weave fabric with particular techniques using specific materials that result in the creation of something which reflects what we like in terms of pattern, colour or shape. It may be a flower, a geometric pattern or simply different stitches that make for surface texture interest.

There is often anxiety about 'techniques' and 'correctness' when doing needlepoint, but there are no *rules,* only lessons to be learned from past masters of the art. What they have passed on to us are what we call 'stitches', which make needlework easier and create certain effects. We need to choose which of these stitches best suit our own work. Many of them, such as cross-stitch, have been in use for thousands of years so there is no mystery surrounding them. If you want to do a particular stitch, then follow the instructions. On the other hand, the way you cover a canvas is entirely up to you and there is no 'correct' way. Some embroiderers work a pattern in meticulous stitches, each perfectly done. Others work rapidly in a simple stitch, such as random long stitch, filling up a large canvas quickly and are impatient with any delay in creating the desired result.

There is a place in all good craftsmanship for genuine pride in what we are doing and the carrying out of the skills involved with attention and care. To make something as well as you can deserves the highest praise.

CHOOSING YOUR PATTERN
The patterns in this book fall into several categories. There is the jewel box of colour and shape in the flowers of the cottage garden; the plants of the hedgerows through four seasons; the harvests of the field and orchard; and patterns inspired by country living.

There are *natural patterns* like 'Victorian Roses' and 'Pot Marigolds' which show flowers and foliage in a natural way; *repeat patterns* like 'Blue Floral Repeat', 'Red Diamonds' and 'Ripe Cherries' where one or two motifs create an overall effect which is very suitable for uphol-stered soft furnishings; and *stylized patterns* like 'Ice Flowers', 'Fishpond' and 'Waterlily', in which plants or creatures are fashioned with little attempt at life-like detail. Then, there are *traditional patterns* which are based on existing embroidery styles, such as the patterns for 'Opus Anglicanum', 'Chasuble Reverse' and 'Unicorn'.

There are also individual flowers and fruit, and these I call *small designs.* Finally, there are what I call *backgrounds within patterns,* such as the trellis effect in the pattern for 'Lady's Bouquet'. If you like one of these background effects, why not use it separately for a needlepoint without the central motif?

PICKING THE PATTERN YOU WANT TO EMBROIDER
The patterns in this book are graphed in colour, each small square representing one stitch. They are very easy to use. Simply count the squares as you stitch. If there is a line of, say, ten blue squares, then do ten blue stitches and carry on in this manner.

Don't rush when making your design choice, for the decision is one you will live with for a long time. The easiest patttern in the collection for the beginner is 'Ripe Cherries'. The most difficult is 'Marbled Paper'. If you grasp why this is so then you will better understand the pattern you eventually choose to work.

'Ripe Cherries' is ideal for the beginner because the number of colours is limited and the fruit and leaves are 'flat' in that they do not have highlights and shadows. Thus, the number of times you change wool colours as you work is less and, most important for the novice in counting stitch patterns, there is less likelihood of confusion in counting squares.

As I became more adept, I felt that I leaned too heavily in favour of patterns which were easy to count and work, and wondered where I could find a real challenge in pattern counting and stitchery? I discovered the answer in old books whose inside covers contained marvellous marbled papers with small silk pieces called 'head bands' at the top. I learned to make marbled paper and, from a successful effort, drew 'Marbled Paper' and 'Head Band' needlepoint patterns in tones of blue, red and brown.

Here are some clues in selecting any pattern – whether a counted one or a printed canvas.

Usually the more colours in a pattern, the more shading and tonal qualities. This can be confusing even on quality printed canvases. The colours of these canvases, like those printed in books, cannot be as subtle or as distinct from one another as the colours of wool dyes. I have seen professional designers of needlepoint kits create patterns of flowers or animals which look wonderful when printed on paper or canvas, but which are almost impossible to work as almost every other stitch is a different colour. It makes heavy going of what should be a pleasure.

How large are the coloured squares on the pattern which you are to follow? If they are much smaller than those in this book, you will strain to keep count and frequently lose your place as you look back and forth from needlepoint to pattern.

How many stitches are to be used? The greater the variety of stitches, the more you will have to note when to change from one to another, in addition to counting squares.

You may wonder at spending so much time on selecting the pattern you are going to work, but the needlepoint will take you many hours and it will last many years, so initial considerations are always important.

REPEATING PATTERNS
There are a few elements about working repeats which are helpful to bear in mind when deciding to do a repeating pattern. Unless the designer has worked out and shown you the space created between the motif you are repeating and how to fill it, then you will need to do something about the new shape that emerges as you work the pattern.

Another consideration is how small or large you want the repeat to be over the entire canvas. The size and number of the pattern shape to be repeated on a canvas involves a number of elements. First, pattern size depends on the mesh size of canvas. For example, 14 to the inch canvas gives a much smaller repeating shape than 7 to the inch canvas, where each shape would be large. Second, how will you use the finished work? Is it to be a bold cushion or a small pretty one? Is the needlepoint to cover a chair or sofa?

Both the object and the place where it will be seen need to be considered. An example of this is 'Blue Floral Repeat'. The pattern worked on 12 to the inch was perfect for a small cushion, but for the Victorian chair the overall effect demanded a bolder pattern. Hence the fabric for the Victorian chair was worked on 10 to the inch mesh. The smaller repeat would have proved too fussy over a large area and from a distance would have lost definition.

GEOMETRIC OR ABSTRACT PATTERNS
Unlike the patterns for flowers and leaves, where a few stitches one way or the other will hardly matter, in geometric designs the formality of the repeat demands exact repetition of each part of the design and the regularity of canvas mesh is ideal for this. Consider the wide range of geometric patterns all around you: hexagons, octagons, combinations of stars, rosettes, squares and pentagons – they all add up to a fresh look for your needlepoint.

BACKGROUND PATTERNS
One of the exciting innovations you can add to a needlepoint is a textured background. Not only can you use a totally different stitch for filling in the background of your work, but you can also make the background a different design as in, for example, a chequerboard pattern which is traditional and simple to do – just stitch small blocks of colour, one light, the other dark. These may be tones of the same shade or two different colours, as long as there is a contrast. Stripes, zig-zag lines and small motifs such as a leaf or a flower are all possible as background. Some examples in this book where you will find motifs that can serve as background designs appear in 'Ice Flowers', 'Head Band', 'Victorian Bouquet', 'Blue Floral Repeat', 'Sweet Rosemary', 'Opus Anglicanum', 'Chasuble Reverse', and 'Snowflakes'. You will probably spot others that can also be used.

BORDERS
Many of the patterns have borders which can be worked separately. You can use them for

The Flowers and Butterflies cushion demonstrates the dramatic effect of using black with this design (pp. 66-7).

another needlepoint design – not necessarily one from this book. Borders give needlepoint a finished look. Even running a line of colour, say three stitches, around a work gives it an air of completeness.

Turning corners with borders and frames can be tricky. It is best to start in the middle of the top of the border and work carefully to one corner, keeping a strict count of your stitches as you go. Then go the other way from the middle to the opposite corner. From that point onwards it is easy just as long as you count the stitches correctly. When you are working leaves or flowers a stitch more or less does not matter, but in repeats, borders and geometrics the object is to start and finish exactly where intended.

Using Part of a Pattern

It is amusing and rewarding to pick and choose what you like from the patterns. You might choose to scatter the bright flowers from the 'Pot Marigolds' pattern at random over a canvas and forget about the pot. The little bird in the large design 'Birds and Flowers' could be used as a motif for a bag. Pick a few snowflakes from the 'Snowflakes' design and ignore everything else.

Working Mediums

Needlepoint can be done in the mediums of wool, silk, or cotton threads and beads on hard or soft canvas. It may incorporate leather, odd bits of fabric, metallic threads like gold or silver, stones, shells, and any objects you may wish to put into your embroidery. If you are including beads, then use one bead per coloured square as if it were a stitch. The patterns in this book are designed with traditional needlepoint in mind, using wool or silk threads on single or double mesh hard canvas. But don't let that stop you from trying other materials.

The End Product

Needlepoint is nothing more than a stiff fabric which can be used, for example, as upholstery, around wastepaper baskets, for a handbag, as a rug or in garments.

Designing Patterns

The English countryside is an inspiration of

Wild flowers growing in a lane near a tiny hamlet called New Invention inspired Graham Arnold to compose this painting of his favourite books, his morning coffee cup, and a scene from a green hill that starts at his backdoor and climbs straight up to the sky.

colour and shape. From a technical standpoint, the patterns were first sketched, then drawn on graph paper in colour, and these were then repeated in finished artwork for the book. If you feel you want to try your own hand at creating a pattern, then all you need to do is get some graph paper and coloured pencils and set to work. Remember each square represents a stitch. It is tricky to create shadows and shading, and not have the pattern turn out 'flat', but the effects you seek can be achieved.

Colour

I think it is colour more than shape or the style of things which entrances us. Choice of colour in charted patterns is one of the creative features of this kind of design. There are no limits on what colours you may choose for a pattern. While I hope that you will like many of the wool colours that I have selected for the patterns in this book I also hope you will decide in some cases that *your* choice is the best one. There are no rights and wrongs as long as what you decide to use pleases you.

In choosing colours, the use of primary colours such as red, yellow and blue enhances visual impact. The embroideries and other folk art of the past used a more limited range of colours which has much to commend it as rich effects can be obtained. Don't forget that black and white are colours too. They can be dramatic and stand out.

The patterns in this book are printed in as bright a colour as possible to make it easier for the eye to follow when counting stitches. The wool colours suggested are more subtle.

Some Colour Terms

The terms *hue* and *shade* are both used when referring to colours. Generally the term hue refers to the colour itself, for example red, while shade refers to the degree of red, for example scarlet or crimson. Shade sample cards showing the colours of yarns available can be bought from manufacturers.

Background Colour

Background colour can bring a definite style to your needlepoint. For example, dark backgrounds such as black, deep green and chocolate brown all have a Victorian feel, while apricots, pinks, pale creams and sea greens all speak of contemporary style. Bright oranges and purples have a definite 1960s ring to them while sludge greens, khaki browns and rose pinks mirror the flat tones of the 1930s.

Colourways and How to Use Them

On each page where a pattern appears, you will find a *suggested* colourways list. The colourways give numbers for both Appleton's Crewel Wool which is coded 'A' and for Paterna Persian Yarn which is coded 'PA'. The colours are grouped according to the major hues. For example, all the reds, pinks and oranges are under the heading 'Reds', while all the yellows, golds and embers are under the heading 'Yellows'. If the colours are for a border then the word 'Border' will appear in the colourways list.

Yarn manufacturers can and do change their ranges, adding and subtracting shades and they can also change the code numbers. If you buy an Appleton or Paterna shade card every few years you will always have correct yard codes to hand.

Remember, the colourways are only my suggestions and I hope you will decide for yourself what colours please you best.

Kinds of Yarn

Needlepoint can be worked in any kind of yarn except the softest knitting yarn which breaks too easily for use on canvas.

Today, there is a wide choice of yarns for working needlepoint. Manufacturers are increasingly marketing a better product in terms of the quality of the wool, the length of the fibres, which affects strength, and the range of colours which are readily available. Leading brand names now produce special needlepoint wools displayed in open cases for easy selection.

However, the yarns which I find the best are Appleton's Crewel Wool and Paterna Persian Yarn and the colourways given in this book are for these two. There is a difference in strand count for different sized mesh canvases between the two types of yarn. The following charts will help you determine how many strands of Appleton's or Paterna yarn you need for the canvas mesh stitches to the inch you are going to work.

Appleton's Crewel Wool

Canvas	Tent stitch strands	Cross-stitch strands
18 single mesh	2	–
16 single mesh	3	–
14 single mesh	3	–
13 single mesh	3/4	–
12 single mesh	4	–
12 double mesh	4	2
11 double mesh	4/5	2/3
10 single mesh	5	–
10 double mesh	5	3
9 double mesh	6	4
8 double mesh	7	5
7 double mesh	8	6

PATERNA PERSIAN YARN

The yarn comes as three strands loosely twisted and these can be easily separated. This table shows the number of appropriate strands.

Canvas	Vertical or horizontal stitches	Diagonal stitches
18 single mesh	2	1
14 single mesh	3	2
13 single mesh	3	2
12 single mesh	3	2
10 single mesh	4	3
5 single mesh	12	9

ESTIMATING YARN AMOUNTS

It is not possible to give exact estimates of the quantity of yarn required for working a particular pattern unless canvas mesh size and the area to be worked are known. Take the patterns with you to the shop when buying canvas and yarn. They can help you work out the amount of yarn and quantity of each colour you are likely to need for the canvas you are to embroider. For the background you should buy enough wool all at once, as any variations in the manufacturer's dyeing between lots of yarn can show up.

CANVAS

Canvas may be of linen, hemp, polished cotton or plastic. Try to buy the very best canvas. Do not pay good money for any that contains irregularities.

Basically there are two types of embroidery canvas, the single thread canvas, sometimes known as mono, and double thread canvas. The mesh of the canvas is the number of threads to the inch. These vary from as fine as 32 threads to the inch up to the very coarse canvas used for rug-making which may have only 4 threads to the inch.

The number of threads to the inch determines the size of the finished pattern. The smaller the mesh, the smaller the design. The larger the number of threads to the inch, the larger the finished design. Some people count the stitches in following a pattern, others count the 'holes' on the canvas. Do whichever seems to work best.

If you have not done needlepoint before from a charted pattern such as the ones in this book, then you might be confused about the pattern grid count, which is 10 squares to the inch, matching your canvas mesh. Whether you choose to do your needlepoint on a canvas of 10, 12, 14, 16 etc. stitches to the inch, it will still match up with the pattern. Here is why: you do exactly the same number of stitches when you work any mesh size. The pattern will simply work out to be smaller or larger overall. *Simply do one stitch for one coloured square of the pattern.* What you are counting as you work are the number of squares which stand for stitches and *not* how many there are to the inch whether it is in the pattern or on your canvas.

Canvas comes in various widths and it is necessary when you are purchasing it to state the quantity, the width and the mesh required. When deciding the correct mesh to use for the design you want to do, you should have a reasonably clear idea of the fineness of the detail that you want. The smaller the mesh, the finer the detail will be of the pattern. The piece will also end up being smaller in the total area it occupies.

TOOLS AND ACCESSORIES

NEEDLES

Blunt needles are used in needlepoint. This avoids the risk of splitting the thread. Such needles have large eyes making the threading of wool easier. They are sold as 'tapestry' needles in shops and size needs to be matched to canvas mesh. Too small a needle causes the thread to wear as you pull it through the canvas and too large a needle displaces the thread and tangles it. Needles should be clean and blunt. If they become sharp in use, discard them and start with a new one.

SCISSORS

When cutting a canvas, use a pair of heavy-duty scissors. Otherwise a pair of sharp embroidery scissors are needed. These have very fine points so you can snip a thread easily without also cutting through a neighbouring one. If you drop or otherwise damage your scissors so the two points no longer fit neatly together, then buy another pair as the purpose of these speciality scissors has been defeated.

If embroidery scissors are used for cutting other materials, including twine and fabric, the two points will quickly spread and not match. If someone is always borrowing your scissors, then hide them in a safe place. It may be your only solution!

THIMBLES
Some like them, some do not and I am one of the latter. When the pushing back and forth of the needle has caused a sore finger, cover it with a sticking plaster and continue working.

TAPE MEASURE
Get one that shows both inches and centimetres. Old cloth measuring tapes stretch as the years go by. If yours is one of these antiques, hold it against a ruler and check it out.

A ruler is also always handy for needlepoint work.

FRAMES
While most needlepoint workers hold the canvas free from any device, there are a number of frames which can be used and which offer certain advantages. There are square or rectangular frames, often called 'slate' frames, which are either held in one hand or placed against the edge of a table. Other similarly shaped frames are mounted on wooden legs so that the whole affair stands on the floor in front of you. The major advantage of a free-standing embroidery frame is that you can work with both hands, pushing the needle through the front of the canvas with one hand and pushing it back with the other. This speeds up the stitchery, keeps the canvas from warping, and means less stretching of the finished work is required. Working with two hands eliminates 'scooping' with the needle – this is when the needle is pushed through a hole and immediately pushed onwards and out the next. It produces uneven surface tension in the yarn and is commonly practised by almost everyone who works their needlepoint without a frame. The problem with most standing frames sold today is that they are flimsy affairs and topple over when in use.

TWENTY USEFUL HINTS
As this is a book of needlepoint patterns and not a craft manual of instruction, here are just a few useful hints.

1 Wash your hands before beginning your work.
2 Have enough light. Daylight is best but lamplight is fine as long as it is strong and directed on to your work.
3 Clean your glasses if you wear them.
4 Sit in a comfortable chair.
5 Use good needles and clean, sharp embroidery scissors.
6 Buy the best quality canvas you can get, preferably polished cotton.
7 Start at the centre of each pattern and work from there.
8 To centre a design, fold canvas and mark on the two bisecting lines.
9 Work the pattern first, the background last.
10 Keep less than 18 inches (45 cm) of wool in your needle at any one time.
11 Try to keep the tension of your stitches even. Do not pull the wool too tightly.
12 Keep the back of the work free of knots.
13 For a dark background use a coloured canvas, not a white one.
14 Use a natural fabric for storing needles. Synthetics attract moisture and rust needles.
15 Use waterproof markers on canvas, not pencil.
16 If yarn twists during stitching, allow needle to dangle freely and the thread unwinds itself.
17 Do not store needlework or yarn in plastic bags.
18 Leave at least two inches unworked canvas around the needlepoint for purposes of stretching and making-up.
19 Keep a notebook – ideas come and go so capture them for future reference.
20 Relax.

STITCH TECHNIQUES

BASIC BEGINNINGS

When you begin, you will feel all thumbs, the yarn is likely to tangle up on the back of your canvas and you will be impatient and probably say: 'I'll never get it right.' But you *will* get it right and, in my experience, this will take less than an hour. It does not matter if your first attempt produces a 'lumpy' looking work that is out of shape. Never mind, every new needlepoint you do will be more accomplished and you will soon forge ahead with enjoyment.

HOW TO START

Cut a length of yarn no more than 18 inches in length. Thread this through your needle. The strongest way to fasten the yarn to begin your work is to tie a knot in the end and take the needle through the canvas from the right side about two inches or so away from the row where you are going to start work. This leaves the knot on the right side of the canvas which is facing you. You cut off the knot when you reach it as you work the stitches. The yarn to the knot will have been gathered in by your stitches and will be fastened securely and is unlikely to pull out. Now, with threaded needle in hand, make your first row of stitches, remembering each 'hole' in the canvas is one square of the pattern.

When you have progressed until the yarn in the needle is getting short, stop and fasten off the thread by running the needle into the back of the previous row of stitches or bring it up on the right side where a later row of stitches will sew it in. Cut off the yarn, thread a new length through your needle and off you go again.

TENSION

Tension is the key to all textile work. It is the balance between the fabric you are working on, the thread you are placing in it, and yourself. If you are nervous, angry or upset, your tension will increase and show up in your work. If you are relaxed, the tension should be even. The most common fault in beginners is to pull too hard as they make each stitch. Tension is always different between needleworkers, whether they are professionals or amateurs. Practice may not make perfect, but it helps. Some people have such even tension that there is no difference be-

tween one stitch and the next. Lucky them, is all I can say. After thirty years I can still spot in my needlepoint work when I was not sufficiently relaxed.

CORNERS AND CURVES

The working of corners, curves and angles is not easy in needlepoint because you are working on even-weave fabric. You can stitch in any way and direction you like, ignoring the threads if you so wish. In practice this leads to twisted and overlapping yarn with areas of canvas still exposed. At best it sacrifices durability for artistic impulse.

SAMPLE STITCHES

Looking at an array of stitches in a book can confuse the beginner at needlepoint, but some researchers in historical needlework claim that when all is said and done there are only 16 stitches belonging to 7 different families and that all the remaining stitches are merely variations on these basic 16. Discerning which stitch belongs to which family is a matter of some study. What makes it all so confusing is that many of these stitches have several names and are often called one thing in England and another in America. For example, *Petit Point* in the United States usually means either English Gros Point or Petit Point on 18 inch canvas or finer, while *Gros Point* or *Quick-point* in the United States usually means either English Gros Point or Petit Point on 16 mesh canvas or coarser.

In addition to showing in this book how to work Tent Stitch (Petit Point), Gros Point, Tramé, Cross-stitch, Half Cross-stitch, Gobelin Stitch, Mosaic, Padded Satin Tramé Stitch, and Reverse Petit Point, I have given two more stitches which are uncommon variations which may amuse you: the Dyer Victorian Cross-stitch and the Luçat Variation Stitch. Below each stitch illustration is a caption which tells you how to do it.

The patterns are designed with the use of either tent stitch or cross-stitch in mind. These two stitches are the traditional ones for doing this type of counted pattern. One of the stitches illustrated, tramé, is done only if you are working in tent stitch over a double thread canvas, so that your stitches cover the canvas and it does not show through.

DYER VICTORIAN CROSS-STITCH

In Berlin Woolwork in Victorian times, the cross-stitch was usually worked in a fashion which gave a very neat, bead-like effect. It is worked over two single threads or one pair of double threads. This stitch covers the canvas as well as most methods of working cross-stitch, but it covers across rather than down the reverse side of the canvas. Anne Dyer, founder of Westhope Craft College in Shropshire, did considerable research to re-discover this technique.

LUÇAT VARIATION STITCH

Jean Luçat was one of France's leading twentieth century designers and weavers. His influence was especially strong in the 1920s. He started as a painter and is credited, along with the French artist Marcel Gromaire, with reviving France's tradition of tapestry weaving at Aubusson during World War II. Luçat did finely detailed tapestry weaving mainly at the standard Aubusson method of 31 threads to the inch. He used a limited spectrum of colours with strong empha-

Embroidery can be brought out in odd moments of leisure to pass the time and, stitch by stitch, a practical end is achieved. The artist, Marcus Stone, called this painting In Love. *As far as I am concerned she looks too composed for it to be true.*

A hen will happily hatch baby ducks. My hen, Mabel, brought up some, refusing only to teach them to swim.

sis on primary colours and his work is easily recognizable by the use of flame-shaped outlines as in his 'Le Chant du Monde' and 'The Owl'. He first started using wool as an art medium by doing needlepoint and his first needlepoint, a copy of a picture, took him three months. So poor that he could not afford to buy the wool, he used scraps left over from other family pieces. He went on to do more needlepoint, using long stitches and few colours on 12 to the inch canvas. His major woven tapestry works may be seen in many museum collections including Paris, Bordeaux, Aix-en-Provence, Arles, Saint-Étienne, Strasbourg, London, Amsterdam, New York, Los Angeles, Philadelphia and Stockholm.

Liberty in Art is nothing to do with quantity; it dwells in the prudent and persuasive use that we make of the means at our disposal and, in short, in the understanding of those means.
Designing Tapestry (1950),
Jean Luçat, 1892-1966

The stitch which I call 'Luçat Variation' is based on the background weave pattern found in many of his works. In needlepoint technique it becomes a combination of a few mosaic stitches filled in with petit point ones.

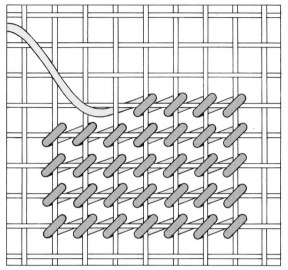

Tent Stitch or **Petit Point.** This stitch is worked on single thread canvas, in rows from right to left, each stitch over one crossing of the canvas, as seen above. Sometimes called 'Continental' stitch in the USA and usually worked below 16 to the inch mesh.

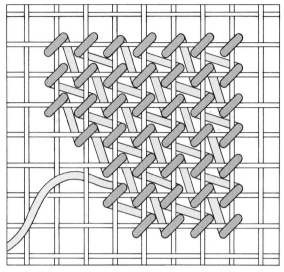

Tent Stitch or **Petit Point** over a large surface is done in diagonal rows, alternately up and down. The diagram shows the upward and downward workings. Sometimes called 'Basketweave' in the USA.

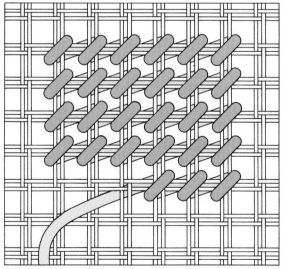

Gros Point, another form of Tent Stitch, is worked in the same way as Petit Point but over two threads in height and width, usually on double thread canvas, in which case go over a pair of threads. Usually done in the USA on canvas above 16 to the inch.

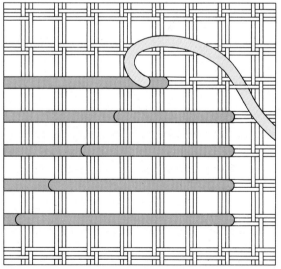

Tramé works best on double-thread canvas. It is useful with Half Cross-stitch. Use the same colour yarns for tramé that you will use over it. Working from side to side, take a long stitch and anchor it with a small back stitch over one mesh. Vary the length of the stitches, otherwise a ridge will appear.

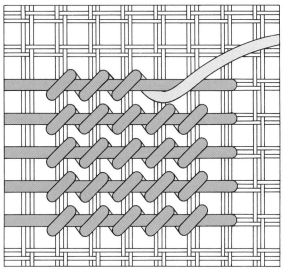

Cross-stitch can be worked in several ways. The simplest is worked in two rows. The first row is done from left to right. Then the journey is made back crossing each stitch to form the second row and complete each stitch.

Half Cross-stitch is worked in rows from left to right and over two threads in single canvas and a pair of threads in double canvas, and over a laid thread (tramé) if the stitches do not sufficiently cover the canvas.

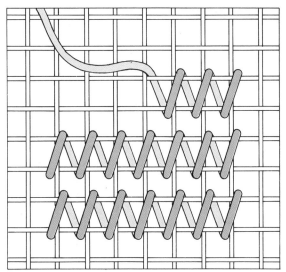

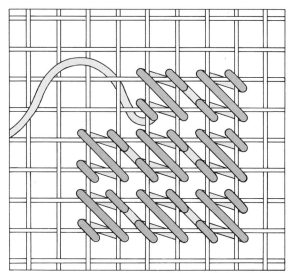

Gobelin Stitch, of which there are many variations, is often used for backgrounds. It goes over more threads in height than in width. It is normally always done on single canvas. Shown here is the Half Gobelin stitch.

Mosaic Stitch, a neat, square stitch which in effect resembles a Cross-stitch. It is useful for background and for shading. Each stitch consists of three diagonal stitches worked over two horizontal and two vertical threads of canvas on single canvas or pairs on double.

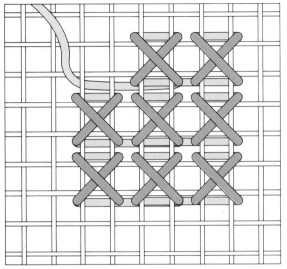

Dyer Victorian Cross-stitch is worked over two single threads or one pair of double threads. While the surface result is similar to Cross-stitch, there is a bead-like effect on the right side and on the reverse side the stitches go across not down.

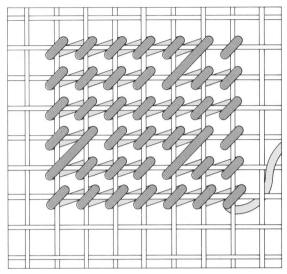

Luçat Variation Stitch is a combination of Mosaic Stitches and Petit Point. The Mosaic Stitches are done at random and the spaces between them filled with the Petit Point. It creates a textured surface when used for working backgrounds.

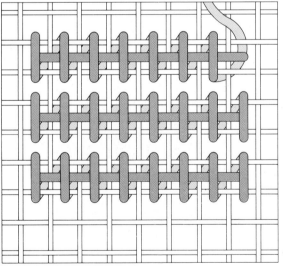

Padded Satin Tramé Stitch. First tram, then do the Satin Stitch. This two-step stitch is good for working both patterns and backgrounds. It covers the canvas completely and makes the needlepoint hard-wearing.

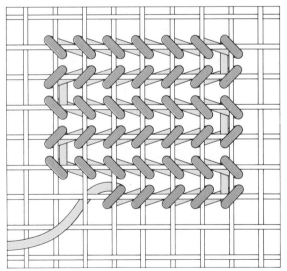

Reverse Petit Point is excellent for creating background interest. It is rather like knitting in appearance and does not warp the canvas, but it is not good for shading.

A Country Alphabet

COUNTRY LIFE

THE COTTAGE GARDEN

Living in the countryside is a modern English day-dream. The things which remind us of this desire to return to rural roots are daily in our lives, from cooking recipes to fashionable reproductions of farmhouse-type kitchens. We are surrounded everywhere by nostalgia for yesteryear. The first step in realizing this dream is to acquire a country cottage. At first the weekends are bliss but then the desire to take up full residence comes like a fever that won't go away. Those who do manage to move to the countryside find it is hard work to get established but rewarding for those who stay the course.

There are hardly any property 'bargains' left in England so what you buy will no doubt turn out to be an expensive 'little gem', but the popularity of owning a cottage down some leafy lane persists as a feature of English life. Human nature being what it is, local folk profitably sell up their ruins, then complain of the lack of cheap housing for the village young. Somehow the former town dweller and the local people contrive to live together. Indeed, much credit for a revival of life in the countryside is due to just this influx of new blood.

The Londoner comes in his big new car;
He thinks what wonderful folk we are.
He takes a walk down the village street;
He finds a cottage that's 'just too sweet'.
He brings an architect, fresh from town,
And the two start pulling the cottage down.

The Londoner comes in his big new car,
He builds a wonderful cocktail bar.
He fills the cottage with chorus girls
In pink pyjamas and paste and pearls.
His pals are rather a pasty lot.
The pearls are cultured – the girls are not.

The Londoner comes in his big new car;
He finds the country too dull by far.
He takes a walk down the village street;
He thinks of the things he used to eat.
Then he calls for his car; he drives away,
And life carries on in the old sweet way.
'Country Cottage', Reginald Arkell, 1882-1959

Morning glories with pink tendrils cover an old stool. I
extended the border of the pattern (pp. 52-3) to fit the area.

Having settled in your country cottage, the next adventure is the garden when town fingers turn green and garden centres flourish.

The first lesson in making a cottage garden is this: the more, the merrier. A cottage garden abounds with flowers and plants tucked into every corner. Some are grand like lilies and lift their scented heads above violets, pansies and columbines. At the rear march the spires of lupins, achillea, delphiniums, sunflowers and pink hollyhocks. All around crowd the climbers and the clingers, like honeysuckle and, as essential as the sunlight itself, there are the many roses, scattering scents and petals into the air.

All this disorder begins with some sort of framework or plan. To start with, a footpath to the door, preferably of stone to keep winter mud at bay. Here, I would first plant violas and alpine strawberries bordering the path on each side. The latter are sweet and give fruit resembling their wild cousin, the wood strawberry. The small heart-shaped faces of violas come in a wide range of colours from the deep pink 'Caroline' to the sombre 'Black Diamond'. 'Susie', 'Pamela', 'Princess Mab' and other viola ladies will give spots of glossy colour along your path.

Beyond this border I would plant in absolutely no order whatsoever: lavender, hyssop, blue flax to wave in the slightest breeze, and big, show-off Victorian Fancy Pansies. So that this little group of delicate colours and painted faces did not get above themselves, I would scatter lots of seeds of pot marigold – brash, hot oranges and globes of lemon yellow – just the thing to make a riot of any careful colour arrangement. There would be columbines, tulips, daffodils, irises, Canterbury bells, 'Cherry Pie', wallflowers, madonna lilies, sweet peas, snapdragons and blue cornflowers. Red, pink and white roses would grow wherever they might, with yellow roses against the brick walls. Large strands of lilac for the spring and wands of butterfly buddleia for the late summer would frame the door to my cottage.

Then, just when you have concluded that this is what your garden grows, you will remember all the favourite plants you have left out. Where are the clove-scented pinks? Or those ancient and dignified old girls – the paeonies – with names like Duchess of Nemours and Sarah Bern-hardt? Aren't there to be some tall phlox or blue campanula or that early Victorian favourite, the Japanese anemone? Is winter to arrive, with all the autumn leaves blown away, without one view of Michaelmas daisies? All these and more will appear in your cottage garden as the years go by for that is how such a garden grows – by gifts from other gardeners and by that irresistible urge that all gardeners know – the need to bring home yet another cutting or plant.

Through the open door
A drowsy smell of flowers – grey heliotrope
And white sweet clover, and shy mignonette
Comes faintly in, and silent chorus leads
To the pervading symphony of Peace.
John Greenleaf Whittier, 1807-1892

In recent years there has been a welcome return to the roses of yesterday and the rich Damask perfume of old shrub roses is once again enjoyed in English gardens. Old-time favourites like fat cabbage roses, moss roses in furry green cloaks, Red Roses of Lancaster and 'Rosa Mundi' in her pink, red and white stripes, make handsome borders. Pink and red roses always inspire needlepoint patterns but there are apricot and cream ones too. Roses like *Rosa rubifolia* with innumerable small flowers bring rich rewards of autumn foliage in red-claret and bronze colours with hundreds of red hips. Old shrub roses require little attention after planting, perhaps a mulch each year in spring and a bit of pruning. Not much for such an annual dividend of beauty.

THE HERB GARDEN

Originally, herbs for medicinal and flavouring purposes were gathered from the wild. There was comfrey (often called 'boneset' and used instead of plaster of paris for setting broken bones), horse-radish, grated and mixed with grease as a hot rub, hoarhound and honey for coughs, and hundreds of other herbal concoctions. The nettles we try to exclude from our gardens were once considered a herb of great benefit. They were used as rennet for cheese-making and for weaving cloth in the medieval days when monasteries were famous for their living 'medicine' gardens.

Today, the widespread popularity of herbs has

ensured that even the smallest garden contains a few. Disenchantment with orthodox medicine and fear of synthetic drugs has turned an increasing number of people to herbal remedies as treatment for simple ills and as tonics for general health. Most cooks want some basic seasonings at hand – rosemary, parsley, thyme, sage and mint at least. Lastly – but surely not least – herbs smell good. In the warm air of summer, essential oils are released as we crush some mint or rosemary between our fingers and happily sniff it.

And thou hast fragrant herbs and seed,
Which only garden's culture need:
Thy horehound tufts I love them well,
And ploughman's spikenard's spicy smell;
Thy thyme, strong-scented 'neath one's feet,
Thy marjoram beds, so doubly sweet,
And pennyroyal's creeping twine,
These, each succeeding each, are thine,
Spreading o'er thee wild and gay,
Blessing spring or summer's day.

John Clare, 1793-1864

Unlike flowers, herbs can be mixed up in a bed and always look happy together. Having picked a sunny open position, make the bed with a raised centre so that the whole bed receives maximum sunshine. Only mint prefers the shade. A bed planted with lovage, chives, marjoram, thyme, summer and winter savory, sorrel, fennel and coriander, with an edging hedge of low-clipped cotton-lavender, will please both cook and gardener. In England, rosemary seems to do best if tied against a wall or planted in a warm, protected place. Good cooks use lots of parsley so a bed of it near the kitchen door makes sense.

Herbs are at home in either cooked or raw fresh salads, although few have retained their popularity through the centuries as much as mint. Spearmint is the one most commonly used for making English Mint Jelly. The homemade kind is more tangy and less sweet than those commercially available. The most deliciously scented of the mints are Apple and Bergamot. These are most valuable in making potpourri.

Both summer and winter savory are aromatic, the first being good boiled with broad beans and both working well as flavouring for lentils. My own favourite herb is borage which scatters its seed everywhere. It is a humble fellow, yet has one of the most beautiful of flowers which is the shape of a star and deep blue. Balm and lemon verbena are both bee plants and one plant of angelica will give you a boxful of short candied stems for a year of cake flavouring and decorating. The smell of angelica when brought into the house is overpowering and I cut and prepare it out of doors.

Sorrel is not very popular in England because it has a rather bitter taste, but a few leaves shredded in a green salad are agreeable, and chopped up it is an interesting addition to soups, omelettes and savoury tarts. Sweet and bush basil are half-hardy annuals so many people will not put them in their herb garden, but they are worth growing for their scent and for use in stews. Hyssop is for salads and broths, purslane for salads or picking. Lamb's lettuce, garlic and chives need no introduction, and lovage can substitute for celery as a flavouring in cooked dishes.

PATTERNS FROM A COTTAGE GARDEN

The first section of needlepoint patterns is divided into plants that climb and cling such as 'Victorian Roses' and 'Morning Glories'; flowers from the border starting with a pot of bright marigolds and ending with stylized scented pinks; and a selection of floral repeats. There are two large repeats, one in blues and one in reds with a 'Carved Head' design such as might be found on an old wooden garden seat or a church pew. Finally, apricot and grey roses and lilies frame and complement butterflies in a Victorian-style design. When you live in the countryside, the way to the gate is almost always through the garden and these patterns are flowers from mine.

CLIMBERS AND CLINGERS

We may think of Victorian roses as stately, planted in formal beds and with grand names like Baroness Rothschild, but in those days there were dozens of other kinds of roses. They happily tumbled about gardens, climbed up walls, pergolas and arches, were gathered in armfuls by grateful housewives, and were imitated in silk and wool in needlepoint cushions, carpets, chairs, bell pulls and slippers. Roses were everywhere for this was the nineteenth-century Queen of Flowers, whose presence is always fragrance and beauty.

Roses have long been popular not just in embroidery but in all art forms. They were an important feature in nineteenth-century fashion, used as a design on cloth for dresses, hats, parasols, trailing evening dresses, even worn in the hair. This popularity seems to have started in the fourteenth century when the flower was used in almost every decorative form – woven, embroidered, painted, carved and printed.

The group of patterns I call 'Climbers and Clingers' includes roses, morning glories, yellow pyracantha berries – and pelargoniums. While violas may live at the rose's feet, the pelargonium is in a pot on my window sill. He is a leaner not a clinger but he is here because I like him so much.

Many admirers of a cottage with its clinging vines and crowd of climbers, hesitate before planting them around their own home in the mistaken belief that such plants will crumble the brickwork, dislodge mortar and generally play havoc. If there were much truth in these accusations, then most of the old cottages would long ago have fallen down. In reality, the right plant put in the right place with the right supports will do well and not much affect your house.

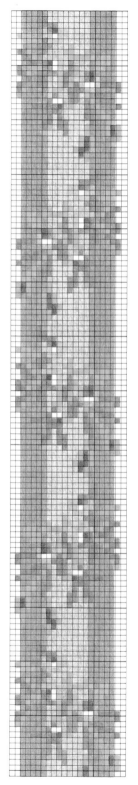

Walls are not, of course, the only place for climbers and clingers. Trellis-work, fencing, arches, pergolas, old trees, sheds, roofs – almost anything will do.

Such plants have different techniques for reaching up and may have tendrils, twining stems, twining leaf stalks, aerial roots, or thorns. If you still don't want to chance putting them on your house, then stick to creating them in embroidery – equal fun and no danger.

The large design is in the Victorian style of plump roses, scattered violas and masses of rosebuds, with a ribbon and pole border to frame the lot. This design lends itself to a firescreen, that practical item once used to protect oneself from the direct heat of an open fire. Old firescreens are easily purchased at local auctions and are usually inexpensive. They do not need to go near a fireplace but can be pretty frames for your needlepoint and placed in a bedroom or hallway. Working the 'rose buds' motif to form a vertical repeating pattern would make handsome matching companion cushions to a firescreen of the 'Victorian Roses' pattern.

COLOURWAYS FOR VICTORIAN ROSES (right)
ROSES: REDS A934, A931, A759, A504, A757, A755, A751 (PA920, PA922, PA900, PA840, PA902, PA904, PA964)   YELLOWS A841, A692 (PA763, PA754)
VIOLAS: BLUES A749, A746, A744, A741 (PA571, PA560, PA561, PA563)   YELLOW A841 (PA763)   RED A931 (PA922)
LEAVES AND FOLIAGE: YELLOW A692 (PA754)   GREENS A407, A404, A354, A353, A293, A343, A345, A347 (PA660, PA611, PA612, PA614, PA650, PA652, PA653, PA603)
BORDER: REDS A934, A931 (PA920, PA922) BLUES A749, A746, A741 (PA571, PA560, PA563)
COLOURWAYS FOR ROSE BUDS (left)
ROSE BUDS: REDS A751, A755, A759 (PA901, PA903, PA905)   BLUES A746, A741 (PA560, PA563)   WHITE A881 (PA263)
LEAVES AND STEMS: GREENS A353, A404 (PA604, PA691)

MORNING SUN

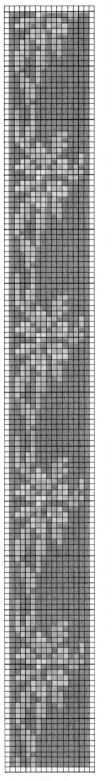

Cheap and cheerful, splashy and showy in the summer garden and in pots anywhere inside or out, pelargoniums and geraniums are the heralds of sunshine. When we decide to move them from window sill to patio, summer is certain to be with us.

These flowers have names which make them familiar and fun – May Magic, Grandma Fischer, Annie Hawkins, Rapture, Godfrey's Pride. I have forgotten the name of the one in my cottage window whose colours inspired me to this large design. I like to think he was the one called Aztec with his Mexican combination of red and pink flowers. For clarity when working the pattern, the dark colours in this design have been lightened. When you see the actual wool shades, the rich contrast between the deep maroon and the pink edging becomes dramatic. I felt that in colour, if not habit, he should be in this design section. As I like adding border against border when working a pattern, I have done a small design in matching colours which I use as a second border. Given enough canvas, I might even repeat the large border yet again – a lush interpretation of the Victorian love of patterns, shapes and colours, piled on to each other.

While you can buy pelargoniums and zonal geraniums in garden centres and most supermarkets, these plants are so easy to grow that from one or two you can create your own pelargonium population explosion with little effort. Take cuttings from February to October only from the last three to four inches of strong stems. Use a very sharp knife or a single razor blade and make the cut just above a leaf-joint. This helps the 'mother' plant. Trim each cutting so it terminates just below a leaf-joint. If you leave a great deal of stem below the leaf-joint, rot may set in and travel upwards into the cutting. Dust the exposed end of each cutting with a

fungicide rooting powder. Do not let a cutting dry out before planting it. Use a garden 'dipper' stick, spoon handle or your finger to make a little hole in a pot of fine soil or seedling compost. Put your cuttings into a pot about 7 to 8 inches (175 to 200 mm) across.

The 'Morning Glories' design returns to the true climbers and clingers – and what travellers the morning glories are, twisting and turning to face the sun with flowers that range in colour from pale blues, deep purples, violets, creams and sky blues to scarlets with bright yellow throats. Morning glories, seen so frequently in nineteenth-century needlework, arrived in England from Latin America. They find happiness in more sheltered spots in the garden along with our very own wild morning glory – bindweed with its small blue-white flowers and its stems twirling about everything, plunging through flower beds, and always triumphant over our best efforts to consider it a nuisance and pull it out.

COLOURWAYS FOR PELARGONIUMS (far left)
FLOWERS: WHITE A992 (PA263) REDS A149, A944 (PA910, PA944)
LEAVES AND STEMS: GREENS A251A, A254 (PA695, PA692)
BACKGROUND: RED A707 (PA865)
BORDER MOTIFS: GREENS A256, A254, A251A (PA690, PA692, PA695) REDS A864, A862, A707, A944 (PA852, PA854, PA865, PA944)
BORDER BACKGROUND: RED A149 (PA910)
COLOURWAYS FOR GREEN AND PINK BAND (left)
STEMS AND LEAVES: GREENS A251A, A256 (PA690, PA695)
FLOWERS: REDS A707, A862 (PA865, PA855) YELLOWS A471, A473 (PA704, PA711)
BACKGROUND: RED A149 (PA910)

COLOURWAYS FOR MORNING GLORIES (overleaf)
FLOWERS: BLUES A747, A745, A743, A741 (PA571, PA560, PA561, PA563) RED A222 (PA932) YELLOWS A474, A471 (PA704, PA726)
STEMS: RED A222 (PA932)
LEAVES: BLUES A747, A745, A743, A741 (PA571, PA560, PA561, PA563)
BORDER: RED A222 (PA932) YELLOW A471 (PA704)

YELLOW GEMS

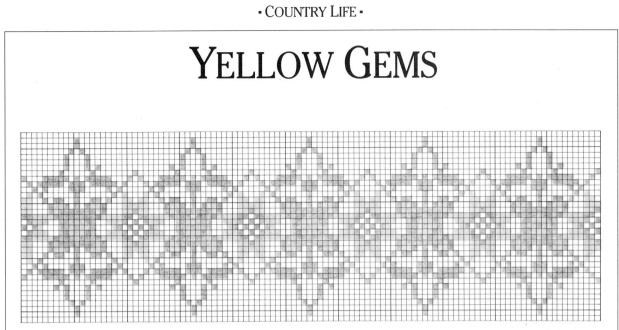

Pyracanthas or firethorns are among the most hardy of garden shrubs. They dazzle with berries of yellow topaz, ruby red, orange garnet and creamy-white opal. One of the best of shrubs, with tough leaves, they are hardy in all weathers and the clusters of tiny white blossoms scent the air in spring.

Let the wealthy and great
Roll in splendour and state;
I envy them not, I declare it.
I rear my own lamb,
My own chickens and ham;
I shear my own fleece and I wear it.
I have lawns, I have bowers,
I have fruit, I have flowers,
The lark is my morning alarmer.
So jolly boys, now
Here's God speed the plough,
Long life and success to the farmer.

Old Saying

While pyracantha can be trained against a wall and the yellow one looks especially good against red brick, an unusual way to place the shrub is to allow a rambling rose, perhaps a copper-pink one like Auguste Gervais to trail through it. Beneath this mass of colour, a low bed of purple-leaved *Ajuga reptans* 'Atropurpurea' would underscore the pale cream and pink picture.

In the large design 'Yellow Gems', the berries of *Pyracantha rogersiana* 'Flava' are treated separately and framed by pale grey leaves. The colours are repeated in the border and the over-all background is the creamy yellow of the plant in flower. The small design 'Floral Rim Motif' is fashioned after one which I found on the rim of a plate. If you want to increase the size of the large design, say for a cushion or a bench, you could use this small motif repeated on the left and right hand side as a final border.

Brave flowers, that I could gallant it like you
And be as little vain,
You come abroad, and make a harmless show,
And to your beds of earth again.

Henry King, 1592-1669

Dealing with the colour yellow, whether in the garden or embroidery, can be tricky. Gold and 'buttery' shades are easy and widely admired in decoration, but lemon and mustard tints present difficulties. Chinese embroideries give us a clue where the imperial brilliance of yellow is toned down by apricots, sky-blues, cream, pink and buff colours. Browns and blacks are used for the opposite effect.

Today our taste runs to soft colours and timidity can lead to room decoration culminating in a boring mono-colour effect, often in shades of pale green or cream. One way to ensure this does not happen is to create a few cushions to add brightness and interest. The Victorians well understood this technique to bring life to a dull room.

COLOURWAYS FOR YELLOW GEMS (left)
BERRIES: YELLOWS A471, A473 (PA713, PA711)   BROWN A696 (PA751)
LEAVES: GREEN A291 (PA534)
BACKGROUND: YELLOW A872 (PA755)
BORDER: YELLOW A872 (PA755)   BROWN A696 (PA751)
GREEN A291 (PA534)   LAVENDER A601 (PA324)
COLOURWAYS FOR FLORAL RIM MOTIF (above)
YELLOW A473 (PA711)   GREEN A291 (PA534)   LAVENDER A601 (PA324)

BORDERS

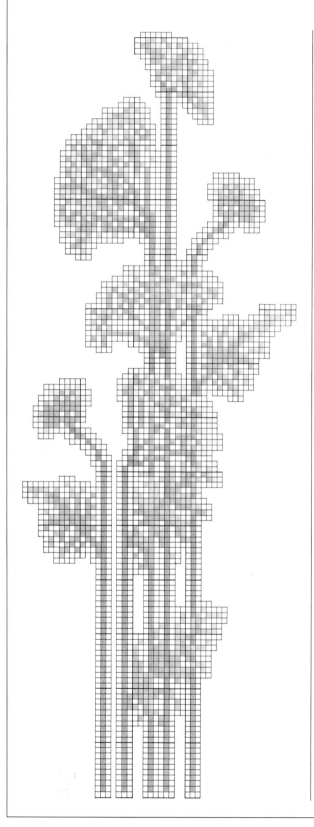

Pot marigolds are probably the friendliest flowers we can plant in our garden and are not to be confused with the stiff little jobs called French marigolds that many, including myself, think stink. No, pot marigolds are of an entirely different ilk, with their bright yellow and orange petals lifting any garden into a scene of high summer. My marigolds last until the first heavy frosts. They set hundred of seeds, scattering colour here, there and wherever around the place year after year. Along with borage, marigolds are easily the most common flowers used in cooking. Some petals in any green salad, especially one which contains segments of orange, are very pretty. As to taste, they have little, if any, as far as I am concerned.

MARIGOLD SALAD

Take 4 cupfuls of cold diced potatoes, 1 cupful of chopped watercress and a tablespoon of chives. Mix together with a cupful of vinaigrette dressing. Stir in 1 cupful of marigold petals, using a few loose petals to decorate the top. Serve at once.

MEDICINAL USES

The medicinal uses of pot marigolds go back a long way – here are a few from 1586:

The juice of the leaves wringed forth and dropped into the eares, killeth the wormes.

The rinde of the Marigold pierceth and digesteth evil humours, which boiled in Wine and drunke, helpeth the stopping and other griefes of the Liver.

The floures of the Marigold stiped in Vinegre and Salt, and reserved, retaine their proper vertue for two years. These comfort the stomack and procure an appetite to meate, yea they consume the humors of the Stomack, and heat a cold breast.

COLOURWAYS FOR POT MARIGOLDS (right)
FLOWERS: BROWNS A697, A183, A185 (PA431, PA750, PA434)
ORANGES A557, A704, A862 (PA813, PA846, PA854)
YELLOWS A552, A551, A844 (PA763, PA713, PA702)
WHITE A991 (PA261)
POT: BLUES A742, A746 (PA505, PA560)   GREY A961 (PA203)
BORDER: BROWN A186 (PA431)   ORANGE: A862 (PA854)
YELLOWS A844, A852 (PA702, PA713)
COLOURWAYS FOR ACHILLEA (left)
FLOWERS: YELLOW A551, A553 (PA763, PA712)
LEAVES AND STEMS: GREENS A545, A544 (PA611, PA613)

SWEET ROSEMARY

No plant has retained its popularity through the centuries as well as lavender. It is easy to grow, possessed of attractive silvery-grey leaves, and has one of the most refreshing of fragrances. Traditionally the flowers are dried and put into tiny cloth bags to scent clothes and linen. One can be put beneath a pillow to induce sleep. Even Shakespeare mentions 'hot lavender' for a head cold – a simple remedy of warm lavender water sniffed to ease the head and awaken the senses.

Pleasant as it is to gather lavender on a sunny day when the scent will circle around you in the warm air, it is best to gather the flowering stems in the morning after any dew has evaporated but before the sun lifts the essential oil from the tiny flowers. The large mauve-flowered varieties are the most highly scented, but there are others whose unusual colours compensate for less scent with pearl-white, pink and rose flowers. In the fifteenth century lavender-scented sugar was considered very special and the 1655 manuscript, 'The Queen's Closet Opened', tells us to pound lavender flowers with three times their weight of sugar.

Rosemary is for remembrance
Between us day and night,
Wishing that I might always have
You present in my sight!
'A Nosegay for Lovers',
Thomas Robinson

If every garden must have some lavender, so it should also possess rosemary. In the large design, 'Sweet Rosemary', bouquets of lavender and rosemary make, as always, ideal companions.

For me, borage flowers are the best blue in the garden. These pretty stars, being edible, can be used to decorate a salad, a cake or other cold food. The flowers and leaves have long been used in wine or 'claret cups', the benefits of which the herbalist John Evelyn noted in 1699 in 'Acetaria, A Discourse of Sallets', 'The sprigs of borage in wine are of known virtue to revive the hypochondriac and cheer the hard student.' The Victorians, making their usual fuss, complicated the recipe but still achieved a fine cool drink:

Dissolve 1 tablespoon of sugar in boiling water, add 1 glass of sherry, half a glass each of brandy and maraschino cherry juice, some thin rinds of lemon and cucumber plus one large bottle of claret. Let the mixture cool. When filling a glass add ice cubes and top with a borage flower.

He who has borage
Will never lack courage.
Old Saying

The small lozenge shape containing the borage flowers may be used as a repeat pattern. The second shape, created as you go along, may either be filled with the background colour you choose or hold a different motif. Borage grows happily in the garden almost anywhere it scatters its seed, so your needlepoint borage will not mind any neighbour you choose for it.

COLOURWAYS FOR SWEET ROSEMARY (left)
FLOWERS: LAVENDERS A101, A105 (PA314, PA312)
LEAVES AND STEMS: GREENS A251A, A256 (PA695, PA691)
RIBBON BOW: BLUE A463 (PA544)
DIAGONAL STRIPE: BLUES A461, A463 (PA546, PA544)
COLOURWAYS FOR BORAGE FLOWERS (above)
FLOWERS: BLUE A463 (PA544)   LAVENDER A603 (PA313)
BLACK A998 (PA221)
LEAVES: GREEN A255 (PA691)
STEM: BROWN A124 (PA484)
BORDER: BLUE A463 (PA544)   LAVENDER A603 (PA313)
BLACK A998 (PA221)

SCENTED PINKS

Lavender, honeysuckle, rosemary and pinks make an excellent formula for fragrance in the garden. The English moist air and temperate climate help to make this special perfume, with pinks and border carnations leading the way with their clove scents.

When rural folk started moving into towns some two hundred years ago, they wanted to recall the countryside and to keep some semblance of it about them. In most cases, they had little option but to put some favourite plants into pots. There were not many to choose from – auricula, hyacinth, tulips, polyanthus, anemone, ranunculus, carnations and pinks. Cotton weavers in the Lancashire mills raised fine auriculas and further north, in Paisley, other weavers bred the first 'laced pinks'. Plant names are often confusing and pinks are properly called Dianthus. This category includes both old-fashioned and modern pinks, alpine and special ones, and border, annual and perpetual flowering carnations. The flowers in my design are cottage pinks – the small ones of garden pot and path.

Garden pinks have green-grey leaves and single or double flowers one to two inches across with either smooth or frilly fringed petals. Pinks are one coloured, bi-coloured with an eye of one colour and an outer area of another, or 'laced' where a second colour forms a loop around each petal. The pinks called 'fancies' wear petals of irregular colours. The pinks you find in my garden and, most likely in any cottage garden, are a variety called 'Mrs Sinkins'.

Thomas Fairchild (1667?-1729) was one of the principal English nurserymen and florists of his time, possessing one of the finest collections of fruits and exotic plants in England. He liked scientific research and hybridization, which was then a new art, and the little pink gave him his first real success. The fact that pollination was necessary to the development of seeds had only recently become established fact and Fairchild was working at an exciting time for plant propagation and development, using scientific methods at the same time as hundreds of new flowers and plants were being introduced from abroad. He became the first person known to have raised a hybrid – *Dianthus caryophyllus* x *barbatus*. His contemporary, the famous horti-culturalist Richard Bradley, said in 1717 the plant was 'neither sweet william nor carnation, but resembling both equally'. The new flower became popular and was commonly known as 'Fairchild's Mule' – that is, neither one thing or another.

The great gardener and plantsman John Tradescant (d. 1638) had discovered wild pinks during his journey to Russia in 1618. On 20th July, 1618 when he first visited Rose Island, he wrote, 'Pinks growing naturall of the best sort we have heere in Ingland, withe the eges of the leaves deeplie cut or jaged very finely.'

Both pinks and carnations remain favourites with the florist trade and the embroiderer. Today, the florist trade calls on these pretty flowers from countries around the world – boxfuls from the British islands of Jersey and Guernsey, brightly coloured ones from Australia, and an entirely new strain of tiny flowered pinks from California. For the embroiderer the choice is just as wide. Motifs of these flowers were done from the sixteenth to the nineteenth centuries, each era offering a different interpretation of leaf, petal and flower. All of them are successful as repeating patterns.

While we in the West have a long tradition of using flowers, foliage, insects and geometric shapes as repeating elements of a design, the use of letters from our alphabet is rarely found in domestic needlework. Yet lettering takes a prominent place among the items of the embroiderers' stock-in-trade. Initials look attractive but why not try out letters as repeating elements. The smaller diamonds in this design could easily have letters of the alphabet substituted for the floral motif. Who knows? – you might work out a secret message.

COLOURWAYS FOR SCENTED PINKS (right)
FLOWERS AND PANELS: REDS A704, A621, A866, A864 (PA846, PA834, PA850, PA852)
LEAVES: GREENS A432, A832, A834 (PA661, PA686, PA662)
BACKGROUND: GREEN A874 (PA605)

FLORAL REPEATS

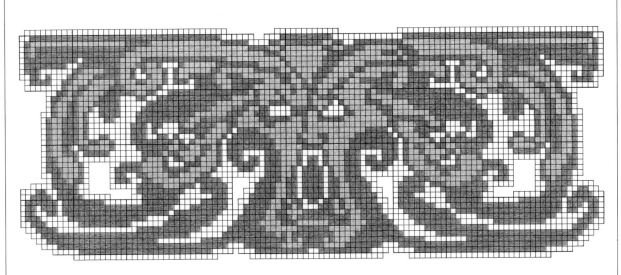

The extensive use of one dominant colour in a pattern brings unity to the design. While the use of naturalistic flowers always looks appealing, stylized floral shapes, like this pattern, 'Blue Floral Repeat' and the one on the following page for 'Red Diamonds', also lend themselves to needlework meant to cover a large area such as a chair or bench.

'Twas midnight – through the lattice, wreath'd
With Woodbine, many a perfume breath'd
From plants that wake when others sleep,
From timid jasmine buds, that keep
Their odour to themselves all day,
But, when the sunlight dies away,
Let the delicious secret out
To every breeze that roams about.

Thomas Moore, 1779-1852

Enclosing each of the repeat motifs is what is called a 'diaper' – a shape not unlike a baby's diaper or napkin just before you fold it around the infant – but one which means something quite different. The word 'diaper' denotes a fabric with a woven pattern which shows up by the reflection of opposing textures in the cloth itself. In fabric ornamentation, such as embroidery, it also means any overall pattern which is capable of extension in any direction for as long as you want to go on making it. For example, this would be true of the 'Blue Floral Repeat' pattern, but not of the 'Carved Head'.

The 'Carved Head' is based on the carved oak panels, pews and stonework found in so many English churches. This pattern is a 'panel' design which means the opposite of 'diaper'. That is, the pattern is confined to a definite space and does not lend itself to being repeated in part or endlessly. You can, of course, repeat it as a whole, but only doing part of it would look odd. Changing a design from the medium of stone or oak, where it is carved, to the almost flat perspective of needlepoint raises problems of shadow and light in order to show curves and depth. For this reason, there needs to be a real distinction between the two shades of colour used. If you choose shades too alike, they will blend and definition of the face and curls of hair will be lost. This design is effective as a border at the top of the large 'Blue Floral Repeat'. It might be a happy combination of the designs if you were covering a straight-backed upholstered chair where the 'Carved Head' would complete the top of the back or form the four side panels of a square stool.

COLOURWAYS FOR BLUE FLORAL REPEAT (left)
FLOWERS: REDS A205, A203, A877 (PA873, PA874, PA327)
BLUES A327, A321, A324 (PA510, PA515, PA512)
FRAMEWORK: GREEN A354 (PA604)   BLUE A321 (PA515)
DIAMONDS: GREEN A354 (PA604)   BLUES A321, A324 (PA512, PA515)   REDS A203, A877 (PA874, PA327)
DIAMOND BACKGROUND: RED A877 (PA327)

COLOURWAYS FOR CARVED HEAD (above)
HEAD: BLUES A747, A745 (PA501, PA561)
BACKGROUND: CREAM A989 (PA236)

RED DIAMONDS

If 'Blue Floral Repeat' tends to be feminine in a Victorian parlour style, then 'Red Diamonds' is Victorian Gothic with a masculine presence. 'Red Diamonds' can be worked as shown or the diamonds moved together which will create further patterns in the space between each diamond. These new shapes which emerge may be filled in with a plain colour, say the pale blue of the diamond. This makes a second repeating pattern. The pattern count will change as you work the diamonds closer together as they do not automatically interlock with each other. Do the first diamond in the centre of the canvas as usual, then work another on the right-hand side. This will show you how they fit. If you need to add stitches or take away some, don't worry. Although it is nice if a repeating pattern *does* repeat exactly over the whole canvas, it need not do so. Small variations add interest and, in any case, too much symmetry can be boring. However, I confess to starting out once to do a needlepoint based on a Persian carpet with the idea of 'just making it up' as I went along. In the end I ripped out the central third of the work a dozen times as it would not repeat correctly. If you are a fusspot, be warned.

A single red diamond could be used as the central motif in a needlepoint, done in cross-stitch, and the remainder of the canvas worked as a plain background in the Luçat Variation or Mosaic stitch to provide textural interest. Another alternative would be to do the single diamond and scatter small plain diamond shapes in red over the surrounding area, with the final background in Gobelin stitch using a pale blue. However you decide to use them, all diamond variations are interesting to work.

Twinkle, twinkle, little star,
How I wonder what you are!
Up above the world so high,
Like a diamond in the sky!
Rhymes for the Nursery, Jane Taylor, 1783-1824

Diamonds are supposed to be a girl's best friend. Most women still find them an acceptable gift, depending on who is doing the giving. The consumer share of diamonds is about 20 per cent of all that are mined, the remainder going for industrial use. If jewellery fascinates you, then you will like the Cullinan Diamond. It was found in South Africa in 1905 and weighed in at a tidy 3,106 carats. If you were born in April, the diamond is your birthstone.

The next design, 'Flowers and Butterflies', returns the patterns to more naturalistic work. This design owes allegiance to Victorian Berlin Artwork patterns and the nineteenth-century's passion for embroidered pieces with a central flower panel and four corners done with the same colours but in swirls of flowers and leaves with curling scroll-work. I have used fairly distinctive colour shades here to distinguish one part of the design from another, but the pattern also lends itself to being worked in colour tones that are so close that definition is lost. The effect of doing this is to create a soft 'antique' look. If you are keen to embroider a cushion that has that old 'yesteryear' feel about it, this pattern is a good one. Simply substitute shades in each colour that are closer and lighter than those given in the colourways. If the suggested black background is changed to a faded cream colour this will also help. This lightening and losing of definition between shapes enhances the effect of age.

The crafts of the jeweller and of the embroiderer have been intimately connected in the past. There was a revival of this practice in the 1950s and 1960s. Beads, of course, are a form of 'jewel' and in the Orient frequent use is made of bits of mirror glass to obtain a brilliant effect.

COLOURWAYS FOR RED DIAMONDS (right)
REDS A504, A505 (PA950, PA951)   GREENS A254, A541, A429 (PA692, PA615, PA620)   BLUE A564 (PA553)

COLOURWAYS FOR FLOWERS AND BUTTERFLIES (overleaf)
ROSES: CORALS A863, A862, A861, A702 (PA855, PA853, PA846, PA854)
LILY: GREYS A964, A989 (PA201, PA202)   PURPLE A102 (PA313)   LAVENDER A884 (PA334)   CORALS A861, A862, A863 (PA846, PA853, PA855)   GREENS A834, A254 (PA690, PA662)
LITTLE FLOWERS: GREYS A963, A989 (PA236, PA202)   LAVENDERS A885, A884 (PA333, PA334)   CORALS A861, A862, A863 (PA846, PA853, PA855)
BUTTERFLIES: LAVENDER A855 (PA333)   BROWN A476 (PA700)   CORALS A861, A862, A863 (PA846, PA853, PA855)   GREY A963 (PA236)   GOLD A844 (PA702)
LEAVES AND STEMS: GREENS A834, A644, A254, A253 (PA690, PA693, PA662, PA692)
BACKGROUND: BLACK A998 (PA221)

VICTORIAN AFTERNOON

Conjure up the warm air of a Victorian summer afternoon, just enough warmth for a damsel fly to glitter like a jewel above a still pond. Down the path from the house are borders heavy with delphiniums and roses, poppies shake out the last petals from their great orange heads, and daisies stand as white as washing on the line. A grey cat hides under cooling leaves of catmint, fragments of leafy scent caught in his fur. The sound of the gravel path beneath your feet is harsh and you step onto the wide lawn where a table is laid for tea. Waiting there is someone you love. Soon friends will arrive, children will run down slopes of tidy grass into the lush orchards. There will be games, gossip, laughter and happiness. As the afternoon draws to an end, memories remain – a straw hat on the grass, a long hair ribbon curled against a white wicker chair, the perfume of roses anointing the far corners of the garden, the whispered words of would-be lovers. Someone still sits under a tree reading poetry in the fading light – perhaps a slim volume of poems by George Massey, the son of a boatman, who, as a child of eight, worked in the silk mills, raised himself up by talent alone but still felt 'All's Right with the World':

Birds sing as sweetly on the blossomed boughs,
Suns mount as royally their sapphire throne,
Stars bud in gorgeous gloom, and harvests yield,
As though man nestled in the lap of Love:
All, all goes right, and merrily, with the world.
    'All's Right with the World',
    Gerald Massey, 1828-1907

The scene that we imagine here was the once idle hours of an English afternoon. In short, the world of manor houses, rectories and the homes of rich merchants. A world created by the wealth of an empire where 'the sun never set', giving birth to a huge middle-class, reigned over by an inaccessible but beloved Queen. This world, for all its pleasured afternoons and pursuit of leisure, was not a lazy one. It was cultivated and mannered, valuing style even more perhaps than

A winter afternoon, a fire burning, and tea with crumpets is a countryside tradition still giving pleasure today.

we do a century later, yet it established much that was practical and of benefit to everyone, such as proper public sanitation – no laughing matter for this did as much to promote general good health and longevity as most of the medical discoveries that have since been made. This new middle-class, always keen to keep up appearances at any price, enjoyed itself. Today, we still have much of the anxiety about wealth or the lack of it as they did. Without forgetting the poverty and moral hypocrisy of those days, we still envy the simplicity and warmly human activities of those Victorians – conversation, games, looking at pictures, reading, painting, taking strolls, pasting-up photograph albums and scrap books, listening to and making music, all the benefits of guilt-less leisure.

Sweet after showers, ambrosial air,
That rollest from the gorgeous gloom
Of evening over brake and bloom
And meadow, slowly breathing bare

The round of space, and rapt below
Through all the dewy-tasselled wood,
And shadowing down the horned flood
In ripples, fan my brows and blow

The fever from my cheek, and sigh
The full new life that feeds thy breath
Throughout my frame, till Doubt and Death,
Ill brethren, let the fancy fly

From belt to belt of crimson seas
On leagues of odour streaming far,
To where in yonder orient star
A hundred spirits whisper 'Peace'.
                                        'In Memorian A.H.H.',
                        Alfred, Lord Tennyson, 1809-1892

Just as English food grew out of a domestic life dominated by women cooks – unlike the French tradition of male chefs – so the Victorian home was the primary source of pastimes and social events. A major mid-afternoon event was tea – not the quickly brewed cuppa, but a ceremony in some respects almost worthy of the Japanese, with white linen tablecloths, teacloths and petite napkins. Many of these linens were of the finest materials and workmanship. Some would be drawn fabric work or 'pulled work', where the various perforations in the material form 'holes' which together make up a pattern, by working certain stitches in such a way that the threads of the material are pulled aside to form an open-work pattern. This technique gives a pretty, lacy effect but does not impair the strength of the material as the threads are not withdrawn from the fabric structure. Another favourite Victorian needlework technique was 'Drawn Thread Work' which creates a delicate webbed effect. Certain weft and warp threads are removed from the material and decorative embroidery stitches added to the threads that are left. 'Drawn Thread Work' encompasses embroidery also known as 'needleweaving' and 'Hardanger'. Nowadays needleweaving has again become popular and the technique is applied to many different types of textile projects to obtain a variety of patterns and effects. Another Victorian way of decorating linens was 'Cut Work'. Here, areas of the material are cut away from the background of the design. In its simplest form, 'Cut Work' spaces are arranged so that each piece overlaps another. Around the edges of these open spaces are sewed a double line of running stitch, which are then covered over by being worked in button-hole stitch – all needing careful and patient hard work. The fabric used in this embroidery technique must be stiff and relatively heavy so that puckering can be avoided. Other familiar embroidery effects on linen such as cross-stitch, appliqué, and *broderie anglaise* were popular with the Victorians.

Today, there is a roaring antiques trade in secondhand linen – the more decorated by needlework, the more costly. Sometimes it can be hard to tell if a particular piece is Victorian, Edwardian or from the 1930s as favourite patterns continued from mid-Victorian days until the Second World War and technical skills remained good. I had the pleasure in Cambridge of being shown a white lawn baby gown of drawn thread, white embroidery and lace worked by Mary Louisa Pearson Sinker in 1929 when she studied at the Royal School of Needlework. It was as fine and as accomplished a piece as anything in a collection from Queen Victoria's day. All such works are family heirlooms and ought to be treated as such. If you have not been lucky enough to inherit some, then do what I have done – save up and buy one or two good second-hand examples or set about trying yourself to create some for your own 'next generation' heirlooms.

Having put a fine cloth on the tea table, the Victorians would have given much consideration to the china, silver and various assorted cakes, crumpets and small sandwiches which were to be eaten. Among the Victorian favourites were sponges – a plain cake with a layer of jam or cream – and madeira cake. Here is the Victorian cook and writer Eliza Acton's recipe, first published in 1845 in *Modern Cookery*:

A GOOD MADEIRA CAKE
Ingredients: 4 eggs, 6 oz (170 g) sugar, 6 oz (170 g) flour, 4 oz (100 g) butter, rind of 1 lemon, ⅓ tsp carbonate of soda.

Whisk four fresh eggs until they are as light as possible, then, continuing still to whisk them, throw in by *slow* degrees the following ingredients in the order in which they are written: six ounces of dry, pounded, and sifted sugar; six of flour, also dried and sifted; four ounces of butter just dissolved, but not heated; the rind of a fresh lemon; and the instant before the cake is moulded, beat well in the third of a teaspoonful of carbonate of soda: bake it for an hour in a moderate oven. In this, as in all compositions of the same nature, observe particularly that each portion of butter must be beaten into the mixture until no appearance of it remains before the next is added; and if this be done, and the preparation be kept light by constant and light whisking, the cake will be as good, if not better, than if the butter were creamed. Candied citron can be added to the paste, but it is not essential.

Perhaps having had our cup of tea and amused ourselves with day-dreams of spending an afternoon with servants scurrying about to see that we are able to *thoroughly* enjoy ourselves, we can turn to the designs which make up this section. I call them 'peaceful pursuits', because I have tried to combine elements of a Victorian leisured afternoon with an essentially Victorian feel in the patterns themselves. Many of them have a direct nineteenth-century heritage such

as the design for a 'Victorian Bouquet' and 'Scroll' based as they are on the style of old Berlin Artwork patterns. Flowers, fancy floral borders, a geometric of 'Tudor Roses' and traditional Victorian motifs are all to be found in this section.

Let not ambition mock their useful toil,
  Their homely joys, and destiny obscure;
Nor grandeur hear with a disdainful smile,
  The short and simple annals of the poor.

The boast of heraldry, the pomp of pow'r,
  And all that beauty, all that wealth e'er gave,
Awaits alike th'inevitable hour.
  The paths of glory lead but to the grave.
  'Elegy Written in a Country Churchyard',
    Thomas Grey, 1716-1771

Heraldry, the system of identifying individuals by means of hereditary devices on a shield, thus recording genealogies of families, is an ancient custom. It was a medieval identification practice of Western Europe that in Victorian days became a hotly desired possession. This is not surprising, considering the Victorians' concern for social distinction and their liking of a definite class structure. My favourite among the devices used in heraldry is the unicorn and I have included a design for one. He is set on a 'bar' which is one of the ways a unicorn would have been shown in a crest or seal. As my front garden is in England but within sight of Wales, I have included a dragon, a symbol of that green sisterland.

The section closes on patterns for fancy pomanders and garlands and that most peaceful of all pursuits, reading, with a new kind of needlepoint design based on the hand-marbled paper found in fine books.

PEACEFUL PURSUITS

While the quality of embroidery in general started to decline in the mid-eighteenth century, needlepoint found a new place in domestic needlework early in the next century when an ever-increasing middle-class found itself with greater leisure. In 1804 when a seller of prints in Berlin issued a coloured needlework design on squared paper, he started a popularity for canvaswork embroidery over other kinds that continues even today. While squared paper patterns in black and white had been available since the mid-fifteenth century, Berlin Art-work patterns, as they were called, came with squares in colour – no more straining to work out which little black square of marks meant which colour. Now, the needle-worker bought wools to match the pattern and got on with it. Between 1810 and 1840 over 14,000 different designs were produced. Yet this new kind of pattern which was normally very complex had one distinctive drawback and that was a creative one: with colours identified in the design, individual choice of colour was inhibited.

Then a sentimental passion of a
vegetable fashion
*   must excite your languid spleen,*
An attachment a la Plato for a
bashful young potato
*   or a not too French French bean!*
Though the Philistines may jostle,
*   you will rank as an*
*   apostle in the high aesthetic*
*   band,*
If you walk down Piccadilly with a
poppy or a lily in your medieval hand.
*   And everyone will say,*
*   As you walk your flowery way,*
If he's content with a vegetable love which
*   would certainly not suit me,*
Why, what a most particularly pure young man
*   this pure young man must be!'*
*   'Patience', Sir William Gilbert, 1836-1911*

The large design for a 'Victorian Bouquet' is in this Berlin Artwork pattern tradition, with lilies – a great favourite with the Victorians – and unsubtle colours which would have been at home in the last century. In writing about colour earlier in the book, I suggested that needleworkers using my designs substitute colours they prefer to those I chose. This is not easy even when you decide to try it. This was brought home to me when a reader of *English Garden Embroidery* said she liked my designs but didn't like my choice of colours. Fine, I said, substitute your own colours. She glowered at me: 'Have you tried it? I did and finally gave up.' After making some soothing comments and hopefully helpful suggestions I thought about her complaint. When I got home, I tried to substitute colours in one of my patterns. It was not so simple, but the solution lies in practice. So, in this book generally and with this Victorian Bouquet pattern in particular, I have confined myself to a few colours – blue for flowers, yellow for foliage – in order that there is one clearly defined pattern where colour substitution is limited and straightforward. Try it.

The small design, 'Scroll', is pure Victorian – complicated, over-decorous and 'fulsome'. How in the world is it to be used and for what is it suitable? Use it on a small mesh canvas for a bookmark or, better still, work the pattern repeated end to end on two pieces of canvas to make curtain tie-backs. Here again, the substitution of colours is relatively simple.

COLOURWAYS FOR VICTORIAN BOUQUET (right)
FLOWERS AND LEAVES: BLUES A875, A461, A744, A746, A749 (PA256, PA546, PA504, PA560, PA571) YELLOWS A996, A843 (PA714, PA743) BROWNS A767, A696 (PA751, PA400)
LATTICEWORK: BLUES A746, A744 (PA560, PA571)
COLOURWAYS FOR SCROLL (above)
YELLOWS A996, A843 (PA714, PA743) BROWNS A767, A696 (PA751, PA400) BLUES A461, A744, A746 (PA546, PA504, PA560)

VICTORIAN JEWELS

Jewels and women are an immortal combination of beauty and greed – youth enhanced by the glow of rubies, old age dignified by gold and garnets, the not-so-comely enhanced by sparkling diamonds, the flirtatious at play with emerald companions. In the nineteenth century women had a responsibility to wear jewels for this was a way of establishing social status and family prosperity. Against a background of middle-class affluence, political stability and the appetite for social betterment, along with fashions which changed often and needed to be maintained, jewellers thrived. Gradually women wore more and more gems as the wealthy and the middle-class could afford to change jewellery with the dictates of fashion. However, very grand jewellery, like inherited tiaras and necklaces meant for state occasions or when meeting royalty, were not changed but locked away awaiting the right event.

Like everything else, there were rules about what and when jewellery was to be worn. Etiquette was all, and this even included the materials and the designs of the jewellery. Coral, pearls, ivory, cameos, lockets, crosses and hearts suspended from ribbons, thin gold chains and semi-precious stones were all acceptable for women of every age. Expensive precious stones and fancy gold ornamentation were worn in the evening. Young women, no matter what their social position, were not supposed to wear grand jewels. Discretion was their lot even at evening events and diamonds were distinctly out of bounds.

Sentimentality is a hallmark of the Victorians, so cameos bought in Italy and little commemorative items such as a locket of a loved one's hair incorporated into a brooch were worn

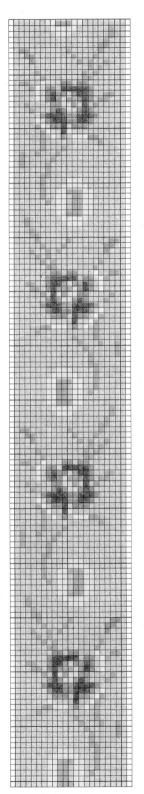

with affection. Many things had significant meanings – such as each flower standing for a sentiment – so it is not surprising that jewellery should also have included messages. Rubies repeated twice, emeralds, garnets, amethysts and diamonds arranged, for example, in a ring to spell out 'regard' with their first letters was a great Victorian favourite.

The following extract is from *The World of Fashion,* September 1844:

'Bracelets are now considered indispensable; they are worn in the following manner; on one arm is placed the sentimental bracelet, composed of hair and fastened with some precious relic; the second is a silver enamelled one, having a cross, cassolette, or anchor and heart, as a sort of talisman; the other arm is decorated with a bracelet of gold net work fastened with a simple knot, similar to one of narrow ribbon; the other composed of medallions of blue enamel, upon which are placed small bouquets of brilliants, the fastening being composed of a single stone; lastly a very broad gold chain, each link separated with a ruby and opal alternate.'

COLOURWAYS FOR VICTORIAN JEWELS (far left)
Jewels: REDS A752, A144, A622, A757 (PA934, PA913, PA834, PA902) BLUE A462 (PA545) YELLOW A471 (PA704) GREENS A333, A256, A251A (PA695, PA691, PA643)
Background: GREEN A298 (PA660)
COLOURWAYS FOR VICTORIAN BORDER (left)
Flowers: BLUES A461, A462, A464 (PA546, PA545, PA543) GREEN A333 (PA643) YELLOW A471 (PA704) RED A622 (PA834)
Jewels: GREENS A333, A256 (PA691, PA643) YELLOW A471 (PA704)
Leaves and Stems: GREENS A298, A256, A333 (PA660, PA691, PA643)
Background: RED A752 (PA934)

PARLOUR REPEAT

Three colours are used in both these patterns. The large design is based on a pattern favoured by both Georgian and Victorian needleworkers for covering large areas such as a sofa, chair or footstool. Once again, the mesh size of the canvas determines the size of the repeat. This, in turn, influences how well the pattern will look on the finished piece. One way to ensure that you balance pattern size to furniture is to work a small area of canvas and pin it to the object to be covered. Leave it there for a few days so that you can study it. When you are quite certain that the shape and size satisfy you, start work on the actual canvas to be used. Changing colours in these patterns offers little difficulty. You might choose blues instead of the green with apricot substituted for the pink, and pale grey for the yellow. Another combination would be greys for greens, blue for pink, leaving the yellow where it is. Trying out various schemes can be fun.

Love is like the wild rose-briar,
Friendship like the holly tree –
The holly is dark when the rose-briar blooms
But which will bloom most constantly?

The wild rose-briar is sweet in spring,
In summer blossoms scent the air;
Yet wait till winter comes again
And who will call the wild-briar fair?

Then scorn the silly rose-wreath now
And deck thee with the holly's sheen,
That when December blights thy brow
He still may leave thy garland green.

'Love and Friendship',
Emily Jane Brontë, 1818-1848

Fancy borders abounded in Victorian needlepoint. This one has honeysuckle as the repeating motif, stylized as it is found in samplers in the early part of the nineteenth century. This small pattern could be used as a border around a cushion in which the central panel is the larger repeat. Alternatively, the border could be repeated in bands across a canvas with a dark green wool between each honeysuckle band – an area of about five stitches should be enough. An examination of Victorian patterns shows that the number of very small borders and motifs was considerable. This is understandable when you see the range of items they decorated – everything conceivable from huge sofas, screens, table rugs and wall hangings to a wardrobe of minutely decorated slippers, collars, coats, waistcoats and hats.

Borders can be used to enclose panels of a great variety of shapes – square, hexagonal, octagonal, circular, or simple geometric forms. Borders may be equally varied in widths even in the same piece of work. Long narrow objects such as tablecloths often have borders wider at one end than the other. Floral decoration in a border is the most common design done, but a most striking effect is a pattern created by a series of different widths of plain colour bands side by side to form a deep border.

COLOURWAYS FOR PARLOUR REPEAT (right)
GOLD A695 (PA752)   PINK A222 (PA933)   GREENS A352, A354, A358 (PA605, PA603, PA610)
COLOURWAYS FOR FANCY BORDER (above)
GOLD A695 (PA752)   PINK A222 (PA933)   GREENS A352, A354, A358 (PA605, PA603, PA610)

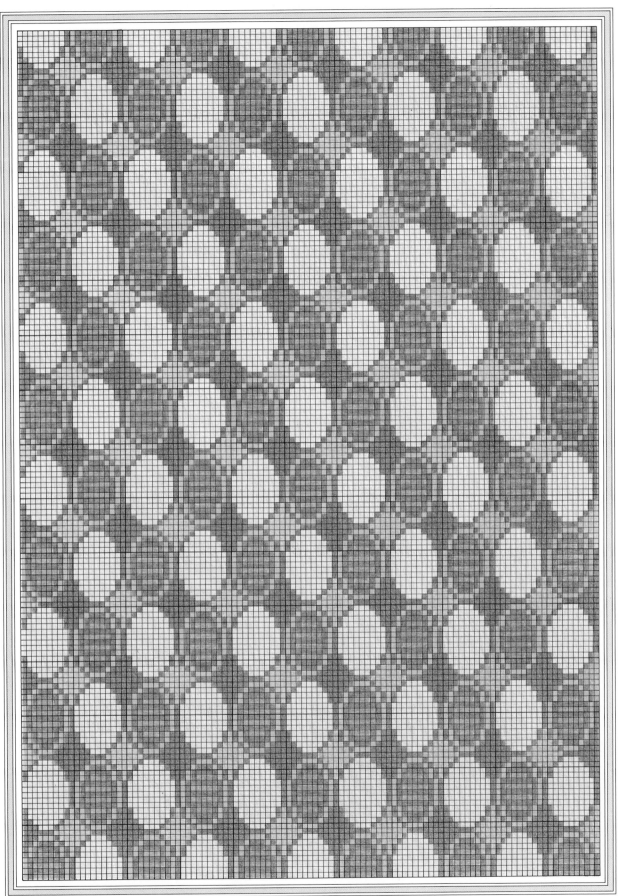

UNICORN

The unicorn, a heraldic favourite, was never very big, rather like an oversized lamb. Folklore has it that the unicorn could only be captured if a virgin was used as a lure. When the unicorn came along and sensed the purity of the maiden, he would run to her and, there, fall asleep in happiness. The unicorn was considered the symbol of virtue and feminine chastity.

The lion and the unicorn
Were fighting for the crown;
The lion beat the unicorn
All round the town.
Some gave them white bread,
And some gave them brown;
Some gave them plum cake,
And sent them out of town.
        Useful Transactions in Philosophy,
            William King, 1650-1729

Medieval writers declared that the unicorn was an arrangement of part lion and part horse with a single horn emerging from its forehead. Artists of that time depicted the creature as multi-coloured – with a white body, a red head and blue eyes. In the thirteenth century, *Le Bestiaire Divin de Guillaume* noted that the unicorn 'has but one horn in the middle of its forehead. It is an animal that ventures to attack the elephant; and so sharp is the nail of its foot, that with one blow it can rip the belly of the beast.' With a creature that was so elegant, so drawn to purity, and yet so potentially fearsome, it is hardly surprising that the unicorn became a religious symbol for Christ himself. As to that dangerous horn, medieval writers soon converted that into symbol easily enough: it was declared to signify the Gospel of Truth. This quaint liking for unicorns has a long history. Ancient classical writers as early as 400 BC described the unicorn as living in India and resembling a white horse but with one long horn which had magical medicinal properties.

In heraldry the unicorn was included in the arms of Scotland and, with the accession of James I, it was combined with the lion in the arms of the British Crown. The Society of Apothecaries, London, has golden unicorns in its device – perhaps representing the fabled medicinal power of unicorn horn.

Everyone is scared of dragons for 'the voice of the dragon is thunder, the trembling of earthquakes his footfall, forest and heath fires are the heat of his breath. He is enormous, and has a scaly body, leathery wings and a forked tongue and tail.' This power to inspire terror made the dragon an ideal candidate as a symbol of invincibility on armorial emblems, especially among Celtic nobility where 'Dragon' was the name for a chief. The dragon of the East is a much nicer chap. He is full of goodness as well as strength, takes treasure into safe-keeping, and likes sun and water.

England retains a fondness for such symbols, and heraldic embroidery of arms, crests and badges is still done for military regiments, colleges, universities and other institutions, as well as for kneelers in churches. These motifs are very decorative and even if you do not have a family crest of your own, the unicorn in this design will look effective as a central panel in a needlepoint.

COLOURWAYS FOR UNICORN (left)
UNICORN: REDS A754, A759 (PA934, PA900)
BAR: BLUES A744, A748 (PA561, PA571)
BACKGROUND: BLUE A875 (PA213)
COLOURWAYS FOR DRAGON (above)
RED A759 (PA900)

TUDOR ROSE

For Victorian gardeners and needleworkers alike roses were bound sooner or later to enter the conversation – whether real lush blooms heavy with scent in the garden or those to be worked in an embroidery. As the Victorians loved their Queen so monarchs through the ages loved the rose as a symbol of royalty and authority. Edward I had a gold one; Henry IV a red one; Edward IV chose a rose with the sun's rays spreading outwards from the petals and known as *Rose en Soleil;* Queen Anne used the motifs of rose and thistle to represent a united England and Scotland; and the Badge of England itself is a rose surmounted by the royal crown. The best known royal rose of all, however, must surely be the one used by Queen Elizabeth I – a Tudor rose with the legend 'A Rose without a Thorn'.

Folklore has it that the Tudor rose sprang from the battlefield on which members of both the York and Lancaster families were slain during the famous 'Wars of the Roses' (1455-85). The name given to this conflict is attributed to Sir Walter Scott in 1829. It derived from the emblems of each side – the White Rose of York and the Red Rose of Lancaster. Peace finally came when the Lancastrians won, killed the reigning monarch Richard II, and Henry Tudor married Elizabeth of York. In this way the two sides were united in the royal family. That union is symbolized in the Tudor rose which combined both the red and white roses.

In heraldry, the dog rose with five petals is used, but for this design four give a symmetrical repeat.

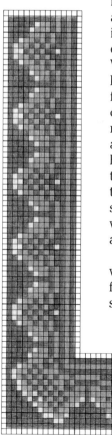

Symbols were not purely the prerogative of royalty for ordinary folk through the ages have used flowers, fruits and animals to declare their special interests or intentions in embroidery. This is particularly so in the working of samplers – those small pieces usually done by children to improve their sewing skills and which are now expensive collector's items. The origins of many of these patterns over the centuries seem to spring from an attachment to symbolic forms by those accustomed to working heraldic and church embroidery. Whether or not the motifs frequently seen in samplers and other domestic pieces held any real symbolic significance is questionable. I agree with those who believe they were embroidered simply because they pleased the eye. Certainly for the little girls working their samplers, each motif gave them a chance to use a different stitch and to improve their colour sense. The following verse, written in the dedication of a book of patterns, still stands as good advice for all who take up needlepoint.

In needle works there doth great knowledge
*   rest.*
A fine conceit thereby full soone is showne:
A drowsie braine this skill cannot digest,
Paine spent on such, in vaine awaie is throne:
They must be careful, diligent and wise,
In needleworkes that beare away the prise.
*   A Booke of Curious and Strange Investions,*
*   published in 1596 by William Barley*

Samplers, particularly the eighteenth-century ones, have an attractive character that springs from the dictates of working on such a regular mesh and from using cross-stitch which also forms a regular surface of squares.

COLOURWAYS FOR TUDOR ROSE (right)
YELLOW A841 (PA763)   BROWNS A765, A183, A186 (PA481, PA434, PA431)   REDS A225, A222 (PA931, PA873)   BLUES A526, A524 (PA521, PA522)

COLOURWAYS FOR TUDOR ROSE BORDER (left)
BROWNS A186, A183 (PA431, PA434)   YELLOW A841 (PA763) RED A225 (PA931)   BLUE A524 (PA522)

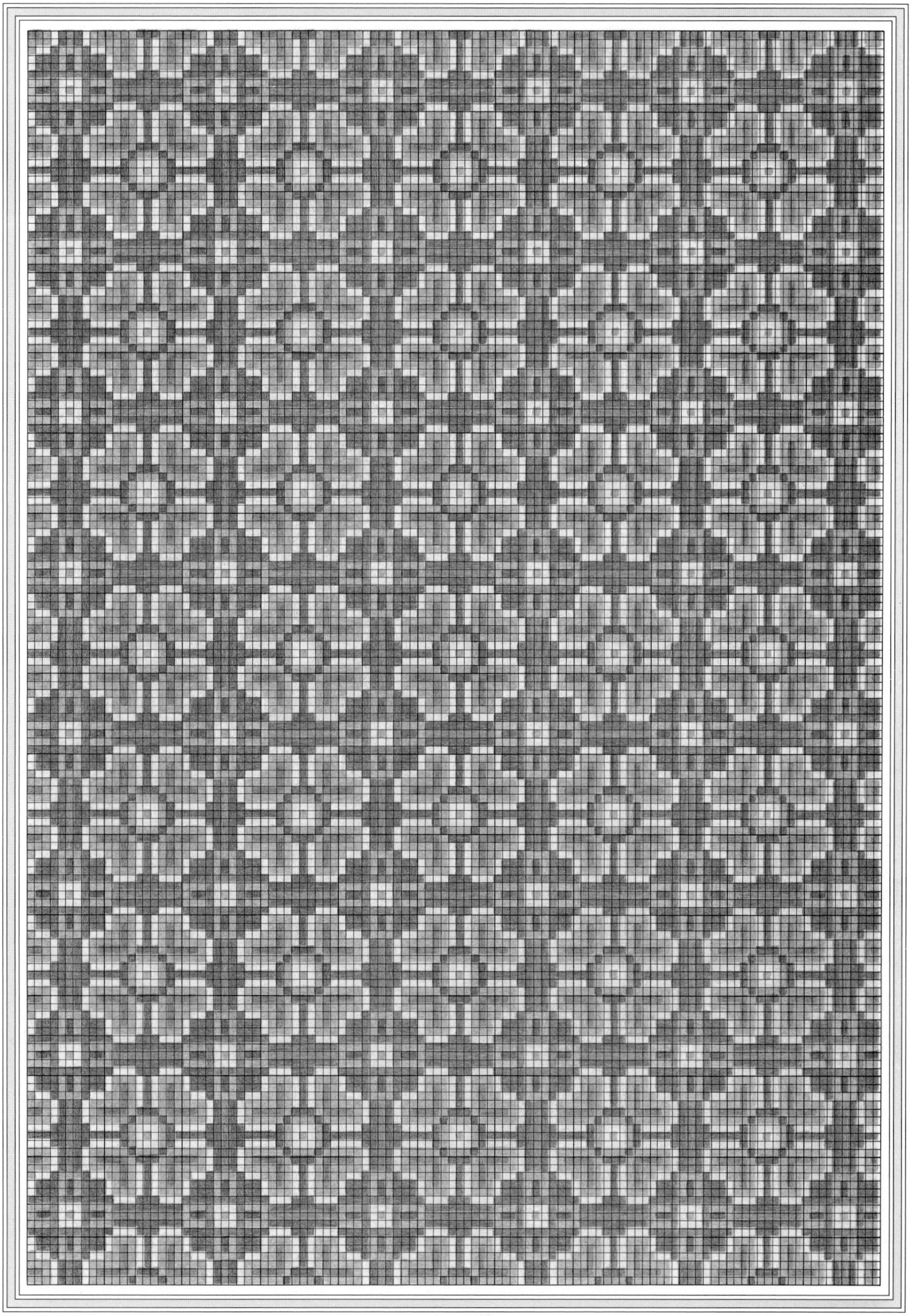

PRIZE BOOKS

In the nineteenth century the printed word not only entertained but provoked emotions, raised beliefs and doubts, created discussion and argument, and stirred the Victorians to new concepts of society and justice to a degree that would surprise us today. As to the novels of those days, we still read with pleasure Brontë, Dickens and Thackeray, to name but three.

'Never judge a book by its cover' may be a wise saying, but some people prize the covers more than the contents for they can be works of art. Even before printing, illuminated manuscripts were bound in a variety of ways with much artistic expression and considerable thought given to their design. The history of embroidered book bindings is a distinguished one. From the fourteenth century until the introduction of morocco leather bindings in the sixteenth century, velvet book bindings were widespread. The Bodleian Museum in Oxford holds a manuscript of 1638 in which the shopkeepers of the Royal Exchange speak of providing 'rare and curious covers of imbroithery and nedleworke . . . wherein Bibles Testaments and Psalm Bookes of the best sort and neatest print have been richly bound up for ye Nobility and gentry of this kingdome, for whome and not for common persons they are indeed most fitt.'

Marbled paper has long been used to decorate both the outside and inside covers of books. The art of marbling is one of those exercises in the mysterious chemistry of different elements meeting each other that fascinates most people – rather like the process of clarifying stock with egg whites. If you want to marble paper, consult a manual of expert instruction but for the idly curious, here is how these beautiful papers are created.

Marbling is the placing of water-based colours onto the surface of a gelatinous sized paper which has a greater surface tension than water alone so that they float. The colours are teased and combed to make a pattern, which is then transferred to sized paper by laying it over the floating colours and lifting it off with the pattern adhering.

It is a craft that is fascinating to try but, as a bookbinder, Paul N. Hasluck, wrote in 1907, 'Though the work is not beyond the capacity of a painstaking and artistic amateur, it will for the majority be found tedious, messy and probably unsatisfactory.'

Marbling almost certainly originated in Persia. It was called *ebru,* which means 'cloud art'. Marbled paper was used in bookbinding in Holland as early as 1598, but it was not actually made in Europe until about 1630. Marbling no doubt came to England soon after this, but the first known English binding with marbled endpapers is a binding of 1655 by Charles Mearne which is in St John's College Library, Oxford.

The original marbled paper on which this complex needlepoint pattern is exactly based was done in my kitchen sink. I made a terrible mess and water flooded the floor, but my nearest neighbour, who *is* a bookbinder, thinks the final result acceptable. As a counted pattern it is the most difficult in this book. The little border is based on matching coloured silks wound around to form a head band which traditionally goes at the top and bottom of quality hand-bound books.

These silk bands are a small detail but a pretty feature of quality bindings. Some bands have two rows with as many as five colours of silk.

COLOURWAYS FOR MARBLED PAPER (left)
BLUE A743 (PA563)   REDS A504, A622 (PA840, PA834)
BROWN A303 (PA483)
BACKGROUND: PINK A707 (PA875)
COLOURWAYS FOR HEAD BAND (above)
BLUE A743 (PA563)   REDS A504, A622, A707 (PA840, PA834, PA875)   BROWN A303 (PA483)

IDLE HOURS

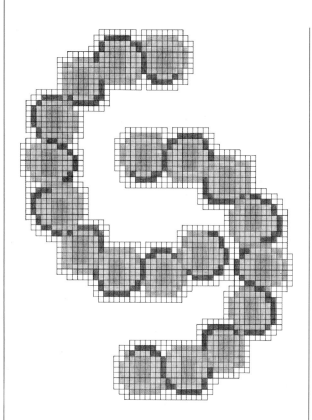

When you tire of taking tea, playing croquet on the lawn, reading poetry, smelling the flowers or whispering to your sweetheart, you can always busy yourself making something nice for the house. Many decorative objects we make today, such as pomanders, were originally conceived for a practical purpose.

In medieval and Elizabethan times, when bad smells and deadly infections were hard to avoid, people turned to herbs and spices for help. The wealthy carried little pomanders made from gold or silver filigree and filled with spices, while ordinary folk made theirs from oranges or apples stuck with cloves and rolled in spices.

To Make a Pomander

Choose an orange and stick cloves all over it in a random fashion. If you have problems sticking them in, use a knitting needle. At the top end of the orange insert a short piece of bent wire to which you can tie a ribbon when the pomander has been dried. If you get too tidy-minded and stick the cloves in neat, straight rows, the orange will split and you will have to start again. Having

stuck in your cloves and the wire at the top, roll your orange in a mixture of equal parts of ground cinnamon and orris root until it is thickly covered. Carefully wrap the orange in tissue paper and store it in a warm dry place for 2–3 weeks until it has dried.

Shake off the excess spices and keep these to use again. Decorate your pomander with a pretty ribbon and hang it up in a linen cupboard or give it to a friend. If you dry it too quickly the orange will shrivel too slowly and it will mildew. I have tried making apple pomanders but they look very unattractive. Oranges are a better bet.

Decorating the house with flowers was a favourite amusement with Victorian ladies. The flowers might be fresh, dried, or fakes made in silk, felt, wax or embroidery. The wax or fabric floral arrangement with a stuffed bird stuck in it and covered with a glass dome is a Victorian conceit which we, thankfully, have not revived. But dried flowers remain highly popular.

Another pastime still done is pressing flowers. Suitable materials range from wild flowers to exotic greenhouse plants, and may be gathered at all times of the year. Composite flowers can provide exciting new shapes when the florets are separated and pressed individually. A telephone directory provides a satisfactory means for pressing flowers as the pages are thin and absorbent. When a variety of dried flowers and leaves has been accumulated, a coloured card, a tube of clear glue, and a small paint brush or tweezers to lift the flowers when arranging them are all the tools needed. A small touch of glue under the centre of the flower or leaf will secure it.

COLOURWAYS FOR POMANDERS (right)
Pomanders: yellows A841, A551, A694, A696 (PA716, PA773, PA753, PA751)
Bows: greys A989, A962, A964 (PA236, PA203, PA201)
Rope: reds A223, A504 (PA953, PA840)
Ribbon: oranges A623, A626 (PA833, PA830)
Border: reds A223, A504 (PA953, PA840) greys A989, A962, A964 (PA236, PA203, PA201) yellow A551 (PA773)
orange A623 (PA833)
COLOURWAYS FOR GARLANDS (above)
yellow A693 (PA734) red A413 (PA923) blues A158, A155 (PA531, PA533)

BEYOND THE GATE

HEDGEROW WALKS

A walk down the long lanes of the English countryside where flowers, berries, wild roses and honeysuckle mingle together makes you glad to be alive. There are primroses and hawthorn in the spring, honeysuckle and elderflowers in summer, blackberries and tinted leaves in the autumn and glossy hedgerow holly for Christmas wreaths. In the English countryside, this green world of forgotten plants and places is just beyond the garden gate.

From my cottage gate, a small wild moor stretches out in every direction. For centuries no plough has touched it. Along one side a river roars in winter, floods in spring, and relaxes into cool pools for swimming in the summer when brown trout rest in the shade of grassy banks. Willows, which the locals call 'sallies', twist and turn over the water, bending into curious shapes. One becomes a low bench where I can rest on my walks. The moor blows with long wild grass and thistles, and the sheep are buried in waves of yellow and green. On the opposite side of the moor runs a small stream, a calm place for moor-hens and ducks, where a heron may silently lift into the sky, his grey wings slowly cuffing back air.

At the far side is the gate into the lane. The rotting doors of a nearby deserted barn reveal dusty hay. Then past the neighbour who keeps pigs. Here bantam roosters as brave as Roman soldiers watch while their speckled hens flap into the ditches to hide. An army of geese, refusing to budge, stick out their tongues with righteous indignation. Then there may be the pigs. You might think they had simply escaped into the lane but you would be wrong. While everything is done to satisfy the Ministry of Agriculture, these pigs have a more natural life than mere regulations might suggest. Three or four baby pigs squealing in the hedgerow and a big sow waddling about and rooting her snout in the earth are not after escape but good health. When a pig feels unwell, it is let loose to find that particular herb which 'cureth best' – and cure it does, for these pigs are always in fine fettle.

This rug pattern (pp. 94-5) has colourways based on the Victorians' love of bright, acid colours, so the actual wools will look far more vivid than in this photograph.

Having passed this orchestration of animals, there is a long stretch of meadow where a cosseted Arabian stallion looks the other way with disdain. After a few more cottages the lane stretches onwards by fields of grain and grass and nearby hills deep with woods.

I crossed a moor, with a name of its own
And a certain use in the world no doubt,
Yet a hand's-breadth of it shines alone
'Mid the blank miles round about –

For there I picked up on the heather
And there I put inside my breast
A moulted feather, an eagle-feather –
Well, I forget the rest.
'Memorabilia', Robert Browning, 1812-1889

Spring has finally arrived for me when there are snowdrops by the deserted cottages. Later in the year these overgrown gardens will yield a harvest of greengage plums and pink apples. Wasps, birds and passing strangers will taste some of this fruit but most of it falls back into the earth to nourish another crop. Sometimes there are cattle in the fields, real Europeans of cross-bred stock with soft fawn English faces and fine French coats, full of curiosity and buzzing with swarms of flies. The cattle stay put, but the flies follow you down the lane. A small branch of elder is an effective switch to keep them away from your face. The perfume of meadowsweet rises into the air.

Rose bay willow herb and mauve foxgloves stand immovable in the stillness. White nettles and coltsfoot flank your feet, blackberry and honeysuckle tangle in bloom and the endless hedgerows on either side delight the senses with colour and smell. You are alone but not lonely nor afraid of the sudden and silent void within yourself. The world is as still as a rabbit who waits by the hedge and, for a moment, you are no longer a child of time.

My little part of England, this magical place of river, moor and lane stays the same because it is remote, but romantic notions about it can soon turn into winter despair when you are snowbound. Another reason there has been so little change is that much of the area is still owned by a family who have lived here for centuries.

Improvements and necessary changes to the land are made, but with care and an admirable slowness that says much for their love of the countryside.

In summer, when the days were long,
We walked, two friends, in field and wood,
Our heart was light, our step was strong,
And life lay round us, fair as good,
In summer, when the days were long.

We strayed from morn till evening came,
We gathered flowers, and wove us crowns,
We walked mid poppies red as flame,
Or sat upon the yellow downs,
And always wished our life the same.

In summer, when the days were long,
We leapt the hedgerow, crossed the brook;
And still her voice flowed forth in song,
Or else she read some graceful book,
In summer, when the days were long.

And then we sat beneath the trees,
With shadows lessening in the noon;
And in the sunlight and the breeze,
We revelled, many a glorious June,
While larks were singing o'er the leas.

In summer, when the days were long,
We plucked wild strawberries, ripe and red,
Or feasted, with no grace but song,
On golden nectar, snow-white bread,
In summer, when the days were long.
'Summer Days',
Wathen Mark Wilks Call, 1817-1890

Here is what I gathered from the lane and the surrounding fields last year: apples and plums for jellies; elderflowers for wine; sloes for gin; blackberries for jam; hedgerow violets and snowdrops for the fire mantel; and wild strawberries by the bowlful. In addition, numerous plants, most of which are generally thought of as weeds, were picked for salads or used for herbal teas.

Natural and herbal medicine has gained much ground with the general public in recent years and some of the most common weeds may help to relieve your aches and pains. Fat Hen – also known as goosefoot, dung weed and dirty dick – is a weed of considerable importance with a name not easily forgotten! It has long been claimed to contain iron and protein and more vitamin B_1, B_2 and calcium than raw cabbage. This once-prized vegetable of the Anglo-Saxons only went out of fashion when spinach was introduced in the sixteenth century. Fat Hen may be cooked like spinach or leaf beet: cut the stems off, chop the leaves, cook over a low heat with butter, season with salt, pepper and a little nutmeg. When cooked, press out excess water and serve with more butter. As in the case of nettles, the butter makes the dish palatable. Young seedlings of Fat Hen are good in salads, and the seeds were once harvested for drying and grinding into grain.

The following is a short list of plants that grow in my lane which, following instructions on use from a good modern herbal, are just waiting to help me over most complaints from bruises to boils. I don't know if dandelion tea actually helps my liver but, sweetened with honey, it soothes my temper.

WEEDS TO RELIEVE YOUR ACHES AND PAINS

Abscesses: Chickweed, Ground Ivy, Yarrow
Asthma: Coltsfood, Nettle
Boils: Chickweed, Ground Ivy, Yarrow
Billiousness: Dandelion, Groundsel
Bladder disorders: Couch Grass, Dandelion, Horsetail, Nettle
Bronchial complaints: Clover, Coltsfoot, Ground Ivy, Nettle, Sow Thistle
Catarrh: Clover, Ground Ivy
Chapped or rough skin: Groundsel
Colds and chills: Coltsfoot, Nettle, Yarrow
Complexion disorders: Dandelion
Constipation: Chickweed, Dandelion, Groundsel
Coughs: Clover, Ground Ivy
Cystitis: Couch Grass
Dyspepsia: Dandelion
Eye lotion: Chickweed
Eczema: Dandelion
Feverish colds: Yarrow
Flatulence: Clover, Dandelion
Foot discomfort: Silverweed
Gallstones: Couch Grass, Sow Thistle
Gout: Couch Grass, Dandelion, Ground Elder, Nettle
Hair conditioner: Nettle, Yarrow

Inflammations: Dandelion, Horsetail
Kidney disorders: Clover, Couch Grass, Dandelion
Liver upsets: Dandelion
Measles: Yarrow
Nervous disorders: Clover
Obesity: Chickweed
Rheumatism: Couch Grass, Ground Elder, Nettle
Sciatica: Ground Elder, Ground Ivy
Skin eruptions: Dandelion, Horsetail
Sore throat: Cinquefoil, Nettle
Stomach upset: Chickweed
Varicose veins: Daisy

Each season brings a different style to the hedgerows. There are more flowers, leaves, plants, stems, foliage, berries and blooms to put into designs for needlepoint than anyone could ever use. From the fields come patterns of pale barley. From the orchards apples, cherries, plums and berries. From the shadow of the woods, the strawberries that remain my favourite embroidery motif.

In spring, even before leaves unfurl and plants begin to grow, the snowdrops and daffodils come out, but, most of all, spring is about birds. With so many hedges and trees still bare, bird-watching becomes an easy game. My first designs from the hedgerow include birds – not any particular kind, just some yellow and grey ones from memory and imagination, shaped like sparrows, cheerful as robins, and busy eating. Summer is the season of smell – meadowsweet plumes float above cow parsley, white and pink May bloom with perfume, and honeysuckle trails its arms everywhere. Then autumn brings a cape of new gold. Finally, the drifts of snow, branches hung with flakes of ice lace. The two miles of hedgerow lane from my cottage is an angelus rung four times a year by nature to the glory of ordinary life.

SPRING

Marsh marigolds, green tints in the hawthorn hedge, ladybird beetles found in unexpected places, little jewels of crocus and mornings filled with songbirds – all this speaks of rebirth. Late April and May are the months of true surprise when blackthorn loosens it blooms, wasps awake, dog violets are at our feet, and swallows are joined by cuckoos, warblers and swifts. Within only a matter of a few days, my lane has turned into a prolific celebration of chestnut and ash in flower and butterflies and bees hungry for the first nectar. The mud may stay underfoot until June, but what does that matter when your eyes are drawn constantly up to the valleys of green hills.

For winter's rains and ruins are over,
* And all the season of snows and sins;*
The days dividing lover and lover,
* The light that loses, the night that wins;*
And time remembered is grief forgotten,
And frosts are slain and flowers begotten,
And in green underwood and cover
* Blossom by blossom the spring begins.*

The full streams feed on flower of rushes,
* Ripe grasses trammel a travelling foot,*
The faint fresh flame of the young year flushes
* From leaf to flower and flower to fruit;*
And fruit and leaf are as gold and fire,
And the oat is heard above the lyre,
And the hoofed heel of a satyr crushes
* The chestnut-husk at the chestnut-root.*
                               'Atalanta in Calydon',
            Algernon Charles Swinburne, 1837-1909

Spring is the season when we declare ourselves unfit, put away the winter's sedentary work, and embark on a programme of exercise – usually involving moving furniture about, annoying everyone by spring-cleaning, and resolving to clear the attic or storage cupboard but never quite managing to do it. There is one bit of clearing up that you should *not* do and that is your needlework box or cupboard. Throw nothing away. There are always bits of fabric and wool, the odd needle, some scraps of cloth or canvas that may come in handy 'on the day'. Do not worry when you find several unfinished needlepoint canvases – every good embroiderer has a basket full of incomplete work which I call 'embroideries of good intention'.

For this design and the next one, I have combined those two harbingers of spring – flowers and birds. These patterns are complementary, using a similar palette of colours. The design with two birds eating berries surrounded by a deep border is ideal for a small rug. The style is Victorian, especially the scrolled border and the use of birds and foliage, but the rose-red and light green colours are much more of our own time. For the background I have used a dark green wool. If you are attempting to make a rug Victorian in feel, then the background should be deep green, chocolate brown or black. Do remember when making a needlepoint rug to use a table to drape the work over as holding the whole canvas will quickly tire your hands.

Compared with many leisure activities, making a rug is an inexpensive project. For example, carpet wool can be bought direct from carpet factories at a saving over prices for needlepoint yarns. The cheapest is thrums but the strands must be long enough for working in flat stitches. To ensure you have sufficient of any one colour to do both ends of your rug, divide each colour into two lots when you begin working the pattern. Add a different colour if you think one will run out.

COLOURWAYS FOR SPRING (right)
BIRD: GREYS A964, A962, A989 (PA201, PA203, PA236) BROWNS A904, A475, A693 (PA441, PA700, PA734) WHITE A992 (PA262) BLACK A998 (PA221)
LEAVES AND STEMS: GREENS A874, A422 (PA665, PA623) REDS A995, A946, A944, A942 (PA950, PA942, PA944, PA933)
FLOWERS: GREENS A874, A422 (PA665, PA623) YELLOW A472 (PA703) REDS A995, A946, A944, A942 (PA950, PA942, PA944, PA933) BROWN A904 (PA441)
BORDER: YELLOW A472 (PA703)

COLOURWAYS FOR BIRDS AND FLOWERS (overleaf)
LEAVES: GREENS A874, A422 (PA665, PA623) REDS A995, A946, A944. A942 (PA950, PA942, PA944, PA933) WHITE A992 (PA262)
BIRDS: BROWNS A904, A475, A693 (PA441, PA700, PA734) GREYS A964, A962, A989 (PA201, PA203, PA236) WHITE A992 (PA262) BLACK A998 (PA221)
BACKGROUND: GREEN A298 (PA660)
BORDER: REDS A995, A946, A944, A942 (PA950, PA942, PA944, PA933) GREENS A874, A422 (PA665, PA623) BROWNS A904, A475, A693 (PA441, PA700, PA734) GREYS A964, A962, A989 (PA201, PA203, PA236) WHITE A992 (PA262) BLACK A998 (PA221)

SUMMER BOUQUET

Summer is the endowment paid for by winter, a reward for our hope and prudence. The hedgerow is heavy with fragrance now – dog roses hang through thick foliage, meadowsweet blankets earth and air; cow parsley still stands tall with creamy heads; grass as red as blood brightens the verges; foxgloves cluster in groups of three or four, dainty gossips in this prolific theatre of green. Some of the weeds are already heavy with seeds. Everywhere birds, rabbits, beetles and bugs feast.

In summer's mellow midnight,
A cloudless moon shone through
Our open parlour window
And rosetrees wet with dew.

I sat in silent musing,
The soft wind waved my hair:
It told me Heaven was glorious,
And sleeping Earth was fair.

I needed not its breathing
To bring such thoughts to me,
But still it whispered lowly,
'How dark the woods will be!'
'In summer's mellow midnight'
Emily Jane Brontë, 1818-1848

The hedges are as tall as the roofs of the deserted cottages and shadows darken the lane. Here, the air becomes moist with humidity and the smell of ripe luxuriant growth. Mosquitoes and gnats hurry to your bare arms and neck. Now you walk quickly, wanting the sun again and the safe innocence of light and summer day-dreams.

Garlands of honeysuckle hang over and through the hedgerow, and the pattern I have designed shows the honeysuckle flowers in yellow and pink although they come in many more colours. I found the following combinations on a single morning: white, pale yellow and cream; white, bright yellow and pale green; yellow and dark pink; cream and red; and some in pink, cream and apricot. You could use any of these

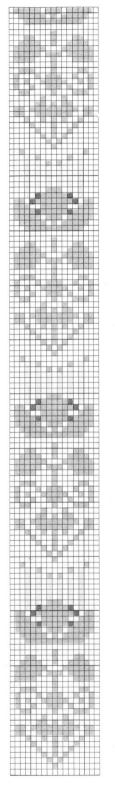

colour combinations if they are more pleasing to you and still be well within nature's own scheme for this sweet-scented plant. Nature may surprise with her colour combinations but she rarely fails to please us.

What is this life if, full of care,
We have no time to stand and stare.

No time to stand beneath the boughs
And stare as long as sheep or cows.

No time to see, when woods we pass,
Where squirrels hide their nuts in
grass.

No time to see, in broad daylight,
Streams full of stars like skies at night.

No time to turn at Beauty's glance,
And watch her feet, how they can
dance.

No time to wait till her mouth can
Enrich that smile her eyes began.

A poor life this if, full of care,
We have no time to stand and stare.
'Leisure',
William Henry Davies, 1871-1940

If you started out in spring to wake up body and soul and maintained resolutions of weight and work, you probably will have succumbed by the time summer days are at their height, and rightly so. For now is the time to pause, to smell, to stare and to enjoy the earth's fruitfulness.

COLOURWAYS FOR SUMMER BOUQUET (far left)
FLOWERS AND LEAVES: REDS A752, A224, A715, A504, A711 (PA932, PA950, PA934, PA914, PA910)
GREENS A242, A354, A241, A356, A253, A254 (PA600, PA693, PA603, PA643, PA692, PA644)
YELLOWS A473, A551, A872 (PA755, PA714, PA703)
WHITE A992 (PA263)
BACKGROUND: GREEN A874 (PA605)
COLOURWAYS FOR HONEYSUCKLE (left)
FLOWERS: RED A224 (PA932)   YELLOWS A473, A551 (PA703, PA714)
LEAVES: GREEN A356 (PA600)

AUTUMN POSY

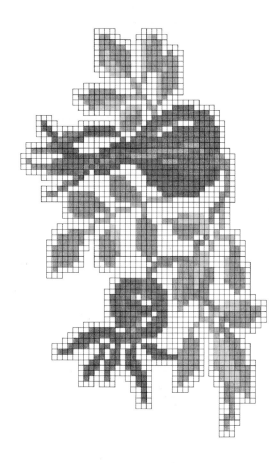

on the glories of garden and nature, should have so neglected the prolific and brightly coloured rose hip.

Tell me not here, it needs not saying,
  What tune the enchantress plays
In aftermaths of soft September
  Or under blanching mays,
For she and I were long acquainted
  And I knew all her ways.

On russet floors, by waters idle,
  The pine lets fall its cone;
The cuckoo shouts all day at nothing
  In leafy dells alone;
And traveller's joy beguiles in autumn
  Hearts that have lost their own.

On acres of the seeded grasses
  The changing burnish heaves;
Or marshalled under moons of harvest
  Stand still all night the sheaves;
Or beeches strip in storms for winter
  And stain the wind with leaves.

Possess, as I possessed a season,
  The countries I resign,
Where over elmy plains the highway
  Would mount the hills and shine,
And full of shade the pillared forest
  Would murmur and be mine.

For nature, heartless, witless nature,
  Will neither care nor know
What stranger's feet may find the meadow
  And trespass there and go,
Nor ask amid the dews of morning
  If they are mine or no.
        (Untitled), A. E. Housman, 1859-1936

Rose hips and sloes are ripe now. Horse-chestnuts fall and hazel nuts must be gathered. The frogs that courted in rainy evenings now begin to retire to winter quarters. Swallows and house martins depart just as the ivy finally flowers. The hedgerow is hung with blackberries. Soon the frosts will start and the lane will roll with morning mist from the moor and the skylarks cease to sing.

Rose hip patterns are among the embroidery motifs I most enjoy working. The small design here could easily be a repeated motif framed by three rows of red wool. The textile scholar, Averil Colby, in her study of samplers, claims that the distinctive rose hip pattern is rare when shown without the rose flower and, indeed, an examination of English samplers over several centuries supports her view. Perhaps there was a prejudice against showing the rose hip separated from its flower. Otherwise, it does seem odd that needleworkers, so anxious to base patterns

COLOURWAYS FOR AUTUMN POSY (right)
BERRIES: YELLOW A872 (PA755)   LAVENDER A104, A884 (PA334, PA312)
LEAVES AND STEMS: REDS A866, A864, A861 (PA855, PA853, PA850)
CIRCLE BACKGROUND: BLUE A875 (PA256)
BACKGROUND PATTERN: BLUE A875 (PA256)   REDS A866, A864, A861 (PA855, PA853, PA850)
COLOURWAYS FOR ROSE HIPS (above)
ROSE HIPS: REDS A148, A504, A502, A944, A751 (PA921, PA840, PA971, PA944, PA964)
LEAVES: YELLOWS A472, A477 (PA703, PA800)
STEMS: BROWN A902 (PA443)

WINTER

Everything now awaits the snow. Starlings roost by the hundred in willows that bend with the wind. Shivering pools of water appear deep within the grass of the moor. The lane lies muddy and naked, waiting for a white gown of sleep. Holly berries fall. Then, one morning, the gate to the world down the lane is closed with icy snow and luminous lights appear on the moor with the rising of the moon. The silence is complete.

Rough wind, that moanest loud
  Grief too sad for song;
Wild wind, when sullen cloud
  Knells all the night long;
Sad storm, whose tears are vain,
Bare woods, whose branches strain,
Deep caves and dreary main –
  Wail, for the world's wrong!
    'A Dirge', Percy Bysshe Shelley, 1792-1822

Lace is very like snowflakes in its fragile patterns and, once you begin to learn to make it, you quickly realize why fine handmade lace has never been cheap – it is a tedious, time-consuming kind of craft, needing concentration and infinite patience. There are many people who discover the appeal of lace but prefer to collect it rather than to make it. Many of the antique lace pieces which are collected are stained and yellow with age. While it may be nice to see these returned to their original whiteness, the process of washing them and using any form of stain removal like bleach damages the fabric of the textile itself. This weakens and shortens its life even more than time will have done. The mellowed effect of age is preferable to damaged lace. Washing of textiles is always an irreversible process so think hard before embarking on it.

While I neither collect nor make lace, I do like the many patterns it forms. I have tried in these two designs, 'Winter Lace' and 'Lace Reverse', to create the look and fragility of lace. While white lace is always attractive I am not keen on using only white in needlepoint, unless a fancy raised or textured stitch is used, such as Rice or Mosaic, to create surface texture interest. Making a new pattern can be quickly achieved by simply reversing what is initially seen. This is exactly what I have done in the 'Lace Reverse' pattern where a single colour, in this case red, unifies the design. 'Lace Reverse' as a background works well but needs careful counting of stitches as you go.

Most needlepoint enthusiasts do a plain ground in a neutral colour – cream, gold, medium green, or light blue being favourites. Yet, backgrounds worked either in a repeating pattern, such as 'Lace Reverse', or in a different stitch from the one used for the main design will bring out depth and texture. Doing a trial piece will tell you if your background ideas work or not.

COLOURWAYS FOR WINTER LACE (left)
BLUE A325 (PA511)   GREEN A403 (PA692)   RED A995 (PA840)
YELLOW A842 (PA773)   BLUE A564 (PA584)   WHITE A881
(PA948)
COLOURWAYS FOR LACE REVERSE (below)
RED A995 (PA840)   WHITE A881 (PA948)

ICE FLOWERS

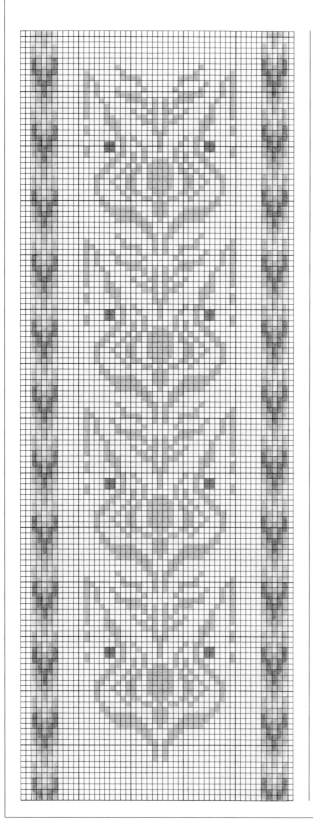

Winter is the time we are glad to stay inside, stare into the fire and dream. It is also one of the best moments to start a new needlepoint. The most comforting sound I know when I am sitting quietly working before a fire in a winter evening, with the dogs silently running in their dreams and the cat staring at some ghostly feline fancy, is the sudden moaning call of an owl. Once, perhaps twice, never a third time – then silence again. The dogs don't wake, the cat's ears flick once, and no one knocks at the door. It is a time when complex details in a needlework pattern are welcomed and concentration on them is a pleasure.

The 'Snowflakes' design reflects these pale days with the lavenders and blues of ice, long rows of mauve and purple shadows, and tiny chains of grey-brown like those that decorate cobwebs on bare hedges. Each snowflake crystal is different in nature, but here just two are repeated to form part of the pattern. Individual ice crystals are endless in variety – needles, plates, prisms and stars. Perhaps it is this imaginative intricacy and unique diversity of pattern that makes each one a miniature work of art. But even a hand held against a window pane will vanquish them forever to watery obscurity.

With such freezing weather, twigs and objects become 'Ice Flowers'. I have organized some into a pattern in which the parallel borders may be worked in Florentine stitch.

How happy is he born and taught
That serveth not another's will;
Whose armour is his honest thought,
And simple truth his utmost skill!
'The Character of a Happy Life',
Sir Henry Wotton, 1568-1639

COLOURWAYS FOR SNOWFLAKES (right)
BLUES A745, A876 (PA213, PA561)   LAVENDER A884 (PA334)
GREY A971 (PA464)   WHITE A992 (PA263)
COLOURWAYS FOR ICE FLOWERS (left)
FLOWERS: PURPLES A606, A603 (PA310, PA324)   GREEN A254 (PA693)
BORDER: PURPLES A606, A603 (PA310, PA324)   GREENS A251A, A254 (PA695, PA693)
BACKGROUND: BLUE A886 (PA213)

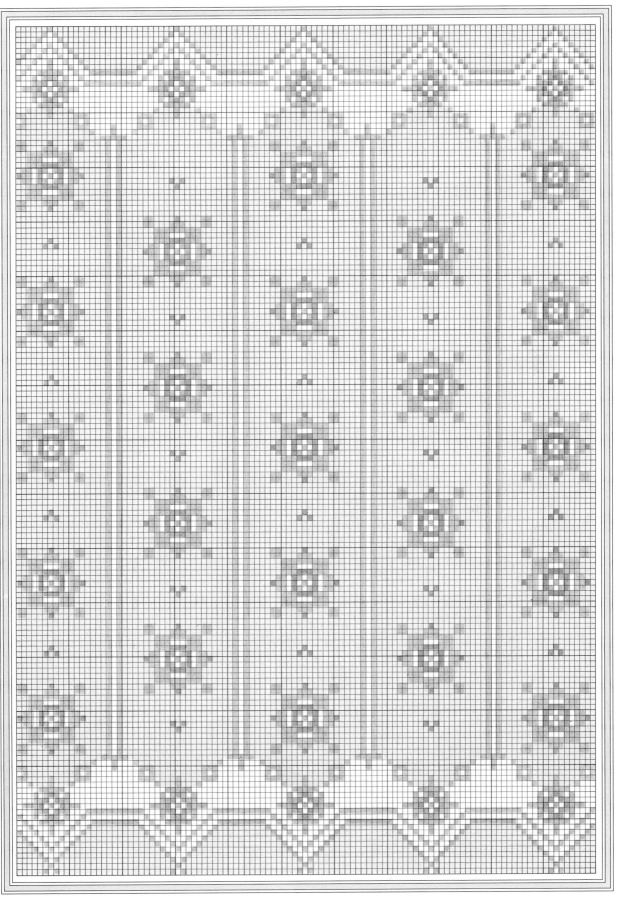

HARVEST TIME

Instead of writing about all the other plants and trees growing down my lane that offer free food, I decided to concentrate on just one – that maligned tree, the elder, *Sambucus nigra*, which grows wild in Britain, and is found in cultivation in America. (American elder, *Sambucus canadensis*, is *not* to be used for any of the following remedies or recipes.)

An English summer has not arrived until the elder comes into full flower, its flat-topped masses of creamy white flowers scenting the air. If it is growing in or near a garden, however, the house owner is likely to cut it down. Even a hundred years ago the Frenchman, Abbe Kneip, deplored how people rooted out the elder 'because every part of it can be used: leaves, flowers, bark and wood'.

Why should there be such dislike? Is it that the ordinary British elder cannot be controlled easily, that its main stems do not grow in an orderly fashion, or do we somehow have an unconscious folk memory of the elder's dark history? Shakespeare refers to it as a sign of grief. Did Judas hang himself from one, as legend has it? Was the Cross of Calvary shaped from elder wood? Folk tales abound – from the old English custom of using elder for funeral purposes to Russia where peasants believed it drove away evil spirits.

Like it or not, elder wood has many uses. It is white, close-grained, easily cut and polishes well. Most important, elder is one of the trees necessary for the proper making of hedgerows.

It is true that elder leaves have an unpleasant smell when crushed and this is supposedly disliked by many insects. Indeed, in the eighteenth century an infusion of the leaves was used on other plants to ward off aphids and caterpillars. Young elder shoots mixed with various sulphates and soap were still being recommended in the 1920s as an effective preventative against fruit-trees blight. What is certain about the leaves is that rabbits and domestic stock avoid eating them and that the bruised leaves, if rubbed on your face, will prevent flies and mosquitoes settling on you.

A work table need not be neat, for bunches of flowers, wools, sketches and books all inspire design (see pp. 75, 119 and 124).

If a compost heap is made under an elder tree, the excretions from the roots, together with the fallen leaves, will assist fermentation, making the compost light and effective in restoring the soil where it is used.

Elder has been termed 'the medicine chest of the country people' and the great physician Boerhaave never passed an elder without raising his hat, so great an opinion had he of its curative powers.

John Evelyn, the English herbalist, wrote in praise of the elder, 'If the medicinal properties of its leaves, bark and berries were fully known, I cannot tell what our countryman could ail for which he might not fetch a remedy from every hedge, either for sickness, or wounds. The buds boiled in water gruel have effected wonders in a fever; the spring buds are excellently wholesome in pattages; and small ale in which elder flowers have been infused is esteemed by many so salubrious that this is to be had in most of the eating-houses about our town.' Elders hold magical powers too. Old folk legend has it that if you stand near 'Mother Elder' at exactly midnight on Midsummer's Eve you can see the King of Elves and all his fabled court go by.

There are a number of uses in herbal medicine for elder. The leaves are a diuretic and a simple tea is said to cleanse the system. The fresh leaves crushed with olive oil relieve the pain of haemorrhoids; the flowers are anti-rheumatic and an infusion is claimed to be good for the throat and voice. Elder bark is a laxative, the berries high in vitamin C – and the Romans used the latter for dyeing the hair.

Ages and ages have fallen on me –
One the wood and the pool and the elder tree.
'Song of Enchantment',
Walter De La Mare, 1873-1956

Elderflower water in great-grandmother's day was for clearing the complexion of freckles and sunburn, and keeping it in a good condition. Every lady's toilet table possessed a bottle, and she relied on this to keep her skin fair and free from blemishes. Its use has not lost its reputation and elderflower water is widely sold today.

Keep beauty and age at bay with some elderflower lotion. You do not need any special equip-ment or skill to make simple lotions or creams, but home-made cosmetics lack preservatives so many of them can only be kept for a short time. Do not let this deter you – if you have the flowers available, try the following recipe.

ELDERFLOWER LOTION

This is made by adding ½ lb (225 g) of fresh elderflowers to a pint (½ litre) of boiling water. Simmer for an hour, then strain through muslin. Add a few drops of eau-de-Cologne when cool if you like, and pour into bottles. This lotion is excellent for washing or for adding to the bath and can be kept for about 3 weeks.

Both flowers and berries have a long culinary history. Here are a few recipes.

ELDERFLOWER CORDIAL

Ingredients: 6 Elderflower heads, 4½ oz (150 g) of sugar, and the juice and peel of 2 lemons.

Place all ingredients in a bowl and pour over 3 pints boiling water. Allow the mixture to infuse overnight. In the morning strain it through a muslin into a bottle. Put the cap on and refrigerate. Leave for at least 2 days. Use as a cordial or as a concentrated base to make up with cold water and ice into a cool drink. The amount of cordial used will vary according to how strong you like it.

ELDERFLOWER FLAVOURING

The aroma of the flowers is so strong that they have long been used as a flavouring for jellies, jams and creams. A bunch of the flower heads drawn through jam or jelly just before bottling it will add a special scent. You may do the same thing with fresh cream after sweetening it with sugar. One or two small heads of flowers tied up in a muslin is a good addition to gooseberries as they cook, but remove the elderflowers before the taste becomes too strong. This combination of gooseberry and elderflowers also works well in making gooseberry jam.

ELDERFLOWER SORBET

Ingredients: 8 elderflower heads, 1½ pints (¾ litre) water, 4½ oz (150 g) sugar and the juice and grated rind of 4 lemons.

Heat water and sugar until the syrup is clear. Remove from the heat and infuse flowers, lemon juice and rind in the syrup for at least 1 hour. Strain. Pour into a metal tray and freeze. When the mixture begins to set, blend and return to the freezer. Repeat twice at intervals to break up the ice crystals. Let the sorbet soften for 45 minutes in the refrigerator before serving.

Elderflower Fritters

Ingredients: 2 dozen elderflower heads, 2 eggs, a pinch of salt, up to ½ pint (¼ litre) milk, 1 tsp melted butter, 4 oz (100 g) flour, oil.

Remove the main stalks, leaving the flowers intact in clusters. Wash them gently in cold water and shake to remove excess moisture. Beat the eggs, mix in the salt, milk and melted butter and gradually blend in the flour to make a smooth batter. Dip the flowers into the batter and fry in deep oil for a few minutes until they are golden. Sprinkle with sugar and serve immediately.

Elderflower Wine

A clear and sparkling summer wine popular among country people until the Second World War.

Place several freshly gathered heads of elderflowers in a deep jar. Pour over 1 gallon (4½ litres) of cold spring water, 1¼ lb (500 g) of sugar, 2 tablespoons of white wine vinegar and the juice and rind of one lemon. Stir till the sugar is dissolved, cover and leave to stand in a cool place for 24 hours. Strain off and pour into bottles with screw tops. Check the tops of the bottles every few days to release any excess 'fizz' which might cause the bottles to burst. It may be drunk in 2 weeks' time, but improves after 6 months.

A little makes a good essence for flavouring cakes and other sweets. It can also be used as a substitute for lemon juice in icing.

Elderflower Vinegar

Take 1 lb (450 g) flowers. Remove stalks from them and dry them carefully. This done, place in a bottle and pour over them 1 pint (half a litre) of white vinegar.

Cork and keep in cupboard. Use after a month, as the flavour lessens with storage.

Many believe that elderberries are poisonous which is *not* true. Elderberries of the *sambucus nigra* tree are delicious when cooked or used in recipes such as those given below. They should not be eaten raw and you must not confuse them with other black or deep purple berries growing in the hedgerows which may be dangerous. Elderberries are ripe when the flowering heads hang down in tassels in early November.

When made into jam or wine elderberries have a distinct 'muscat' wine flavour and smell. In past times, so much local elderberry wine was made that continentals called it 'English Frontignan' after the actual muscat wine.

Elderberry Wine

Ingredients: 5 lb (2½ kg) elderberries, 1 gallon (4½ litres) boiling water, 3½ lb (1½ kg) sugar, 1 sliced lemon, 3 tsp dried yeast, 6 cloves, 2 tsp ground ginger.

Strip elderberries from their stalks and place in a tub. Add boiling water and mash the berries. Leave covered for 3 days, stirring daily. Strain into a pan. Add the lemon and spices. Boil and simmer for 10 minutes. Put the sugar into a jar; when the liquid is cool strain it over the sugar. Put the yeast and 1 teaspoon of sugar into a bowl with a little warm water. When the berry liquid has cooled to blood heat, add the yeast and stir. Put fermentation lock into the neck of the jar. When fermentation ceases, rack and bottle it. The longer you keep it the better.

Elderberry Jam

To every pound of berries (450 g) add ¼ pint (150 ml) of water, the juice of 2 lemons and 1 lb (500 g) of sugar. Boil until set. Put into jars and tie down when cold. Pure elderberry jam is *very* strong tasting and can be sticky. Adding apples to the mixture helps the set and quality of taste.

Ripe cherries, apples and plums, flowers and barley are all in needlepoint patterns for this section. Each reminds us that we are surrounded in the countryside by a rich harvest of good things to eat, much beauty to admire, and nature so inspiring we have taken images of it into our homes through embroidery for a thousand years.

RIPE CHERRIES

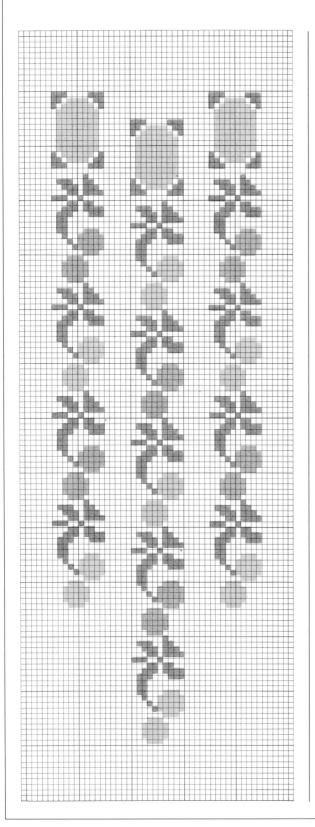

This repeating pattern of 'Ripe Cherries' is ideal for the needlepoint beginner. The number of colours is limited and the counting is easy. No attempt has been made to make the fruit or leaves naturalistic and so any confusion about wool colour shades should be non-existent. If you are new to needlepoint, I suggest starting with this design.

When you have finished the cherries take the pattern 'Greengage Banners' as your next project. Make a cushion square of the banners by doing them in rows down a 10 to the inch double mesh canvas in cross-stitch. Even though you are working them over the entire canvas in long vertical rows, you should still start in the middle of the canvas. Once you have done one row from top to bottom, the remainder will be easy. You will find the count in this pattern slightly more difficult than for the cherries. This should prepare you for your next project which will be to choose any of the other patterns in the book except 'Marbled Paper'. My experience with novices is that by the third time around they are confident about counted pattern work.

The more experienced should not be put off these two patterns; for them the challenge will not be so much in execution but in deciding *how* to use the patterns. Ripe Cherries, being a 'flat' non-perspective design, works well for furnishing fabric, or an individual bunch of the cherries may be used as a motif surrounded by a small frame of three rows of stitches. An alternative for the experienced embroiderer may be to do the cherry pattern not in familiar cross-stitch or petit point but in an entirely new stitch, thus engaging your full attention while new skills are acquired. Another approach would be to work the cherries in glossy cottons, silk or a combination of silk and wool, to give the fruit the natural shine it possesses in life.

COLOURWAYS FOR RIPE CHERRIES (right)
CHERRIES: RED 504 (PA840)
LEAVES AND STEMS: GREENS A253, A545 (PA693, PA692)
MOTIF: GREENS A832, A545, A253 (PA662, PA692, PA693)
BACKGROUND: YELLOW A872 (PA764)
BORDER: GREENS A832, A545, A253 (PA662, PA692, PA693)
BACKGROUND: YELLOW A872 (PA764)
COLOURWAYS FOR GREENGAGE BANNERS (left)
GREENS A253, A545, A832, (PA693, PA692, PA662)

APPLES AND SLOES

Sometimes in autumn when a heavy frost has come to the moor, a crab apple tree, shorn of its leaves, stands decorated like an early Christmas tree with red and yellow apples.

Fair is the world, now autumn's wearing,
And the sluggard sun lies long abed;
Sweet are the days, now winter's nearing,
And all winds feign that the wind is dead.

Dumb is the hedge where the crabs hang
   yellow,
Bright as the blossoms of the spring;
Dumb is the close where the pears grow
   mellow,
And none but the dauntless redbreasts sing.

Fair was the spring, but amidst his greening
Grey were the days of the hidden sun;
Fair was the summer, but overweening,
So soon his o'er-sweet days were done.

Come then, love, for peace is upon us,
Far off is failing, and far is fear,
Here where the rest in the end hath won us,
In the garnering tide of the happy year.

'Kelmscott Crab Apples',
William Morris, 1834-1896

Sloes are the blue-black fruits of the blackthorn which are found in most hedgerows. The fruit is used to make sloe gin by filling a jar with sloes after the first frost and pouring in gin. After two or three months pour off the gin which is now flavoured.

As you might already have suspected, there is a design for elderberries too, so if cooking them defeats you there is always a needlepoint harvest.

COLOURWAYS FOR CRAB APPLES AND SLOES (left)
APPLES: YELLOWS A996, A554, A862, (PA772, PA771, PA854) REDS A502, A995, A716 (PA971, PA950, PA320)
APPLE STEMS: BROWNS A954, A956 (PA730, PA440)
APPLE LEAVES: GREENS A251, A254, A256, A298 (PA694, PA693, PA690, PA660)
SLOES: PURPLES A606, A603, A601, A881 (PA310, PA311, PA324, PA263)
SLOE STEMS: BROWN A903 (PA442)
SLOE LEAVES: GREENS A241, A243, A245 (PA644, PA642, PA640)
COLOURWAYS FOR ELDERBERRIES (right)
ELDERBERRIES: PURPLES A601, A606, A716 (PA324, PA310, PA320)
STEMS: BROWNS A903, A698 (PA442, PA440)
LEAVES: GREENS A243, A241, A254 (PA642, PA644, PA693)

BARLEY

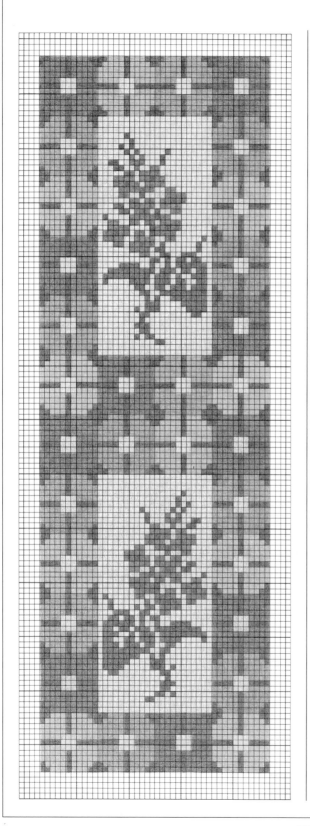

Behind my cottage, the fields are called Cottage Meadows and Top Long Ground. In these fields, my neighbour Frank Goodwin treats the soil as a friend. He practises real farming – the kind that takes effort and thought and doesn't rely on chemicals. He calls it 'good husbandry'. One year the fields may have swedes, another grain, another just grass and rest. This summer there was barley – a coverlet of dusty gold whispering to the wind from Wales and hiding field mice, hares and fat pheasants.

The shepherd now is often seen
Near warm banks o'er his hook to bend,
Or o'er a gate or stile to lean,
Chattering to a passing friend:
Ploughman go whistling to their toils,
And yoke again the rested plough;
And, mingling o'er the mellow soils,
Boys shout, and whips are noising now.
The barking dogs, by lane and wood,
Drive sheep afield from foddering ground;
And Echo, in her summer mood,
Briskly mocks the cheering sound.
The flocks, as from a prison broke,
Shake their wet fleeces in the sun,
While, following fast, a misty smoke
Reeks from the moist grass as they run.
　　　　'February', John Clare, 1793-1864

Beyond the barley other fields stretch clear and clean over the rise in the hill, sweeping upwards to Jay Farm and across to the far lane, where spring brings banks of wild flowers. These are the fertile farms that surround me: not a grand place but felicitous and of good heart. My design is a bouquet of Frank Goodwin's barley, drawn as it was gathered from his Cottage Meadows.

COLOURWAYS FOR BARLEY (right)
BARLEY: YELLOWS A996, A694 (PA773, PA753)　BROWNS A767, A696, A763 (PA402, PA751, PA405)
LEAVES AND STEMS: YELLOWS A996, A694, (PA773, PA753) BROWNS A767, A696, A763 (PA402, PA751, PA405)
GREENS A251A, A241, A244 (PA694, PA644, PA641)
CORNER MOTIF: GREENS A251A, A244 (PA694, PA641)
COLOURWAYS FOR FLOWER PANEL (left)
FLOWERS: RED A224 (PA932)
LEAVES AND STEMS: BROWN A767 (PA402)
BACKGROUND: GREEN A874 (PA665)
BORDER: GREEN A874 (PA665)　BROWNS A694, A767 (PA753, PA402)　REDS A707, A224 (PA875, PA932)

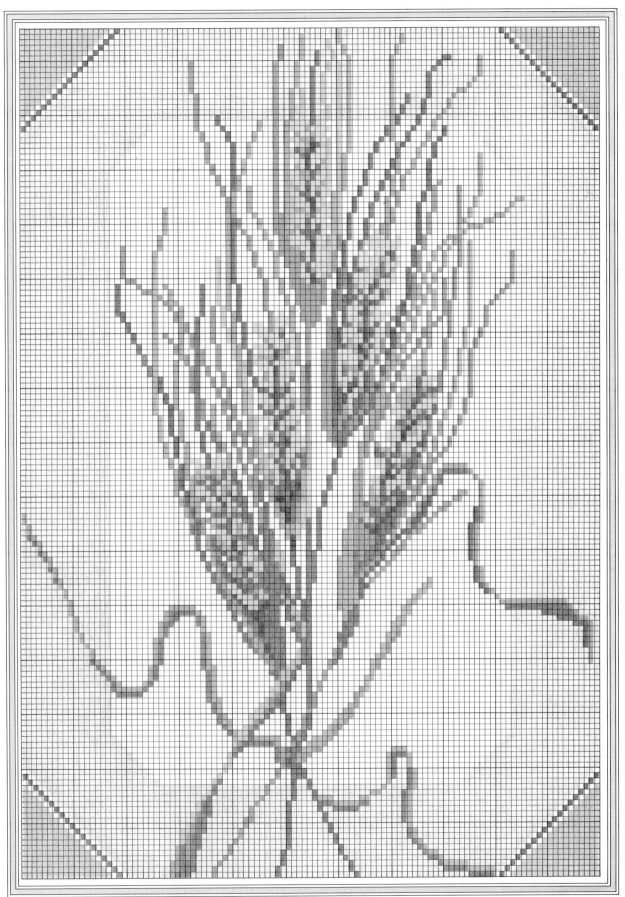

Sunday Morning

Some two miles down the lane from my moor is the village. It is small and ancient. A major road intersects it, yet life continues: the postmaster walks his dog; local women stand waiting for the bus; there is plenty of rumour and gossip; posters in the village shop announce evening classes in a variety of subjects; there is new thatch on a pretty cottage that was once a pub; a blacksmith still works on the corner, the objects of his trade strewn about the place.

Life goes on as it has for nearly 800 years. The church nestles against the yew-topped walls of a garden where there is a ruined castle with a romantic past. New kneelers are being done for the church, each by a different person. Everything inside is in good repair. It would be nice if it were full on Sundays but it hardly ever is.

The rich man in his castle,
The poor man at his gate,
God made them, high or lowly,
And ordered their estate.

Hymns for Little Children, 1848

Even after the middle of the nineteenth century, the concept of a village church and its place in the parish life still held sway but the popularity of science, the organization of labourers into trade unions, and the rapid growth of towns and cities continued to erode the function of the local church as it did the wider style of village life itself. Still, come Sunday morning, as the parson looked out on his congregation he would have noted with satisfaction the local squire, farmers and their neatly dressed wives in their pews, and on benches farm labourers and working folk, the men in embroidered smocks and their wives wearing bright shawls. Illiteracy was widespread so many people would have sat impassively, not there from personal religious convictions but because their employer, the local farmer or the squire, was there. Our notions of how life used to be in English villages are usually more nostalgia than truth. Sunday worship is no exception. People then, as now, were individuals and did not always conform because the local land-

The size of a pattern may be adapted to suit the object to be covered. The cushion, being small, is worked on 12 to the inch canvas. The chair, needing a bolder repeat, is worked on 10 to the inch. The effect is subtle but important (pp 62 and 63).

owner or ministers wished they would. We claim for ourselves a new era of enlightenment about individuality but eccentricity was perhaps tolerated more in the last century, especially in the church. Owen Chadwick in his study *The Victorian Church 1860-1901,* cites George Bayldon who was the vicar of Cowling for over forty years (1850-94). Bayldon was a scholarly man, said to know more than nine languages. He published a dictionary of the Icelandic language, and a history of the Christian church in verse. When he began he was the only man in the village to take a daily newspaper. There was no congregation at all, no Sunday school, no choir. One of the aisles was used for sitting hens. The bell-ringer, a character of notoriety in the village, kept his pigeons in the belfry. Bayldon would go to the vestry, watch from the window to see if anyone came, and if one or two came he might give them a short service with a text and perhaps a few comments on it. If the bishop complained that he had no confirmation candidates, he went round the chapels, got the young to prepare themselves, and took them to confirmation. The parish greatly respected him.

The widespread reading of newspapers was a phenomenon that did not really take place until the last decades of the nineteenth century. Much was changing and the local clergy were at first well to the fore in helping the rural working class organize themselves into negotiating pay and conditions at work. In Leintwardine, a large village a few miles from my home, the vicar helped to found a union of some 30,000 members which negotiated with landlords and had 20 clergymen as vice-presidents. As the century rolled on, church attendance in some places dramatically declined, yet in others thrived.

While it is true that many country churches today are unused and in dire need of urgent repairs, others have been deconsecrated and turned into village meeting places, art galleries, alternative health centres and private homes. The English countryside is still full of church buildings long ago dedicated to man's spiritual quest. Without these lofty spires towering above the landscape, the English countryside would lose that comforting mark of mankind's presence among the greenery of nature.

CHURCH KNEELERS

There has been a revival in making church kneelers. It is work that can be shared out as a community project and this is rewarding. In addition, new hassocks, various cushions and alms bags can be done in needlepoint for the local church. When considering doing a kneeler, it is important that the designs are in keeping with the interior character of the church and its furnishings. Patterns and colour in embroidery can be splendid but not if they clash with the rest of the setting. The first design element to be decided is the theme the kneelers are to take – will it be stories from the Bible, symbols of the church or, perhaps, decorated letters? A theme need not be directly connected to scripture. In our local church, the new kneelers have as a theme the village itself. Each kneeler is a picture of a place in the village. As changes do come about, the kneelers will show a panorama of how the village looks today for the pleasure of the generations to come who will use them. So time spent on talking through and deciding on the theme is well spent. Hopefully, all those who are to do the embroidery will feel happy about the decision.

Designs for the kneelers should be sketched out first, then drawn on graphed paper like the ones in this book. Good working materials are vital as kneelers must withstand hard wear and dirt. Cross-stitch is the hardest wearing stitch and an appropriate one for needlepoint kneelers. Contemporary embroidery designers like using single mesh canvas for kneelers and doing the embroidery in a variety of stitches. The effect is attractive, but not, I think, as hard-wearing as cross-stitch. In any case, surface interest and texture is not what one is looking for in kneelers but rather a design that can be clearly seen when sitting in a pew. Any wording on a kneeler ought to be able to be read from a sitting position above it. The colour used in any wording should also be strong enough so that, even after the fading effects of use and age, the letters can still be seen. Whatever the stitch or the kind of wool you choose, the canvas must be well covered. One major factor in group embroidery of any sort is the varying skills of the participants. For this reason, elaborate designs with fine details are not usually a success. Larger, more geometric patterns or repeating ones are usually a happy choice. One of Britain's outstanding religious and ceremonial embroidery designers since the last war is Beryl Dean. Her books on the subject make excellent preparatory reading before embarking on a church needlepoint project.

In summertime on Bredon
 The bells they sound so clear;
Round both the shires they ring them
 In steeples far and near,
 A happy noise to hear.

Here of a Sunday morning
 My love and I would lie,
And see the coloured counties
 And hear the larks so high
 About us in the sky.

And I would turn and answer
 Among the springing thyme,
Oh, peal upon our wedding,
 And we will hear the chime,
 And come to church on time.

They tolled the one bell only,
 Groom there was none to see,
The mourners followed after,
 And so to church went she,
 And would not wait for me.

The bells they sound on Bredon,
 And still the steeples hum.
Come all to church, good people –
 Oh, noisy bells, be dumb;
 I hear you, I will come!
  'A Shropshire Lad', A.E. Housman, 1859-1936

The inheritance from the centuries of English Christianity is so vast a treasure store that to create only a few designs was a hard decision. I could not resist a pattern based on the wonderful Gothic carvings in wood and stone that adorn so many of England's country churches. The earlier 'Carved Head' pattern is one of these. For this section, I have designed a further two. One is based on Celtic art (page 123) and is a banner of interlocking serpents' heads. The other is a motif favoured during the Roman occupation of Britain: the dragon – that creature of legend who just may have once lived in King Arthur's Camelot days.

From the garden of Turvey Abbey I chose a beautiful Medlar Tree in the last moments of its golden leaves and strange fruit – the very last to ripen in the orchards of England. The tree stands alone at the side of a long path, a golden helmet in the garden.

Time, sunlight, wars and vegetable dyes have yet to fade completely the glory of *Opus Anglicanum* or 'English work' embroidery done for the church from the twelfth to the fourteenth centuries. The goldwork may be bronze with age but the technical virtuosity of its work can still be seen – dark blues are now pale, greens changed to watery blues, but patterns and combinations of colours still delight. The patterns I have designed are based on *Opus Anglicanum* work which is still in existence. They are from priests' vestments called a cope and a chasuble. They are repeating patterns. In the original embroidery, patterns were often repeated over the whole fabric, especially backgrounds. There is always good definition to these motifs and I hope that this element comes through in those I have designed. The original work, of course, was not needlepoint embroidery but wool and silk thread worked on cotton, linen or velvet weave fabric. Metal threads were also commonly used. While colourways are given for wool, there is no reason why you shouldn't try one of these patterns in silk on a fine mesh canvas, say 18 or 22 to the inch. One vertical row of the pattern 'Chasuble Reverse' would lend itself to a bookmark design.

Our prayers should be burning words coming forth from the furnace of a heart filled with love.
                    Mother Teresa of Calcutta

The last pattern in the book, Easter Flowers, is a modest celebration of this spirit.

THE SECRET GARDEN

Past the walled garden of Turvey Abbey where Brother Herbert diligently tends the monastery vegetables, there is yet another garden – a secret one. The way is marked by an ancient Medlar Tree whose wine-coloured fruit ripens only in November, later than any other, beneath an autumn mantle of gold leaves. That other garden lies just beyond the Medlar through a little gate. It is a place of remembrance where lilies float on a fish pond and flowers always seem to be in bloom. Here, one may sit in perfect seclusion and let peace fill the heart.

COLOURWAYS FOR MEDLAR TREE (right)
FRUITS, LEAVES AND STEMS: RED A715 (PA911)   YELLOWS A695, A996 (PA752, PA714)
BACKGROUND: GREY A883 (PA246)
COLOURWAYS FOR WATERLILY (below)
FLOWERS AND FLOWER STEMS: YELLOW A311, A997 (PA743, PA761)
LEAVES: GREEN A354 (PA604)
STEMS: GREEN A311 (PA743)
WATER: BLUES A742, A746 (PA563, PA560)
BACKGROUND: WHITE A992 (PA263)

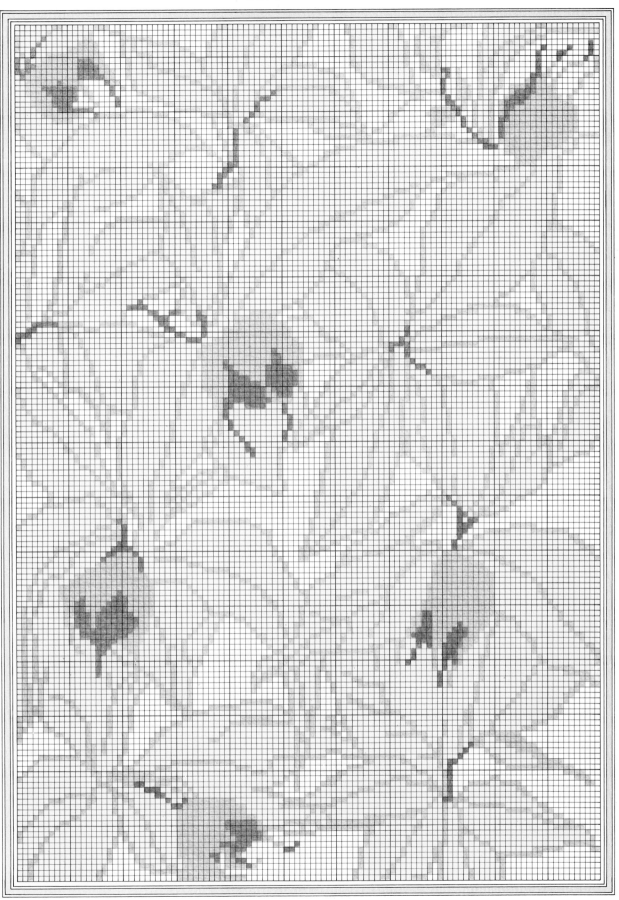

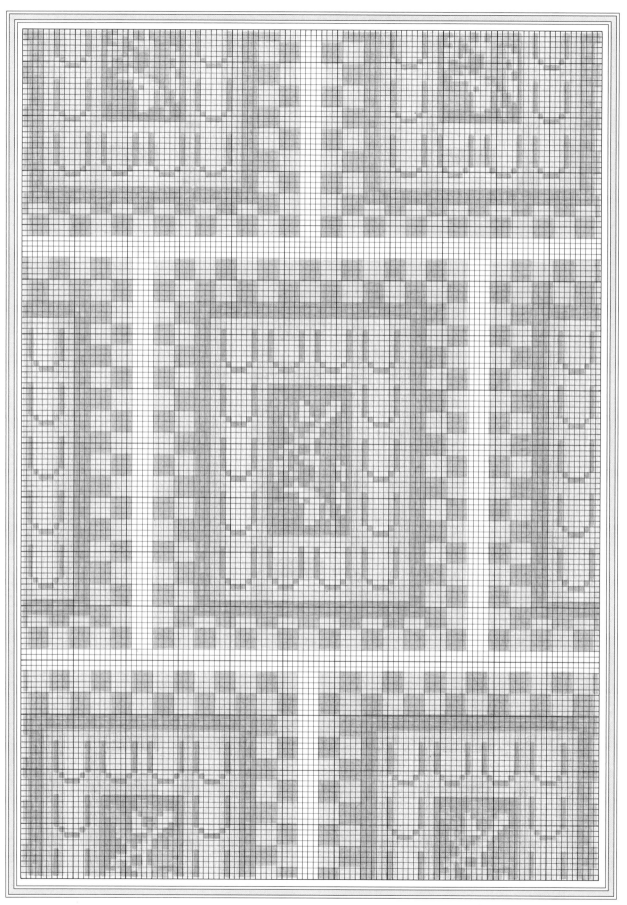

OPUS ANGLICANUM

Among the greatest surviving examples of *Opus Anglicanum* embroidery is the Syon Cope. The cope, a semi-circular cloak worn at liturgical functions, dates from the first half of the fourteenth century. It belonged to the monastery at Syon near London which was endowed by Henry V. When the dissolution of the monasteries took place, this famous cope went with the nuns. They travelled for a number of years through France and Portugal. In about 1810, the nuns returned to England from Lisbon, bringing back with them this cope. Many years later, it became part of the collection in the Victoria and Albert Museum, London. The embroidery is in gold, silver and silks of various colours, and so covers the linen on which it is worked that the fabric is completely hidden. Much of the story of Christianity is in the design – Christ stretching out His right hand toward His mother; the Crucifixion with St John, Mary Magdalene, Saints Peter, Bartholomew and Andrew; and nine of the original twelve apostles can be seen. The Syon Cope is in remarkably good condition and very rare for many such copes were cut up and used for other purposes, not all of which were ecclesiastical.

My design based on *Opus Anglicanum* is inspired from the study of a number of the remaining originals in England and France. The motif is large, incorporating the chequerboard pattern often seen both in *Opus Anglicanum* embroidery and in icon paintings, particularly where garments of the Holy Fathers and Saints of the Church are shown. The 'horseshoe' shape in the motif comes close to what can be seen today in the remains of original embroidered loops and

curves of early ecclesiastical gold work. The faint blue background with an uneven and shadowy effect is an attempt to create the faded qualities of such antique needlework. Finally, the central motif is a floral abstract derived from those found in *Opus Anglicanum*. This seemed suitable in a book about the English countryside where the original embroidery might well have been done.

The one thing necessary for a work of art was that it should bring with it the fertilising seed to come to flower in the beholder's mind: the thought of the artist was to enter like a guest into a room made ready for his welcome.
Laurence Binyon, 1869-1943

Dragons and serpents have long been favourites in embroidery because of legends such as that of St George. They are also old favourites in jewellery design. The small design here is a 'Serpent' motif based on a piece of enamelled Romano-British jewellery. The dragon-like head and its serpent body are abstracted but still discernible.

COLOURWAYS FOR FISHPOND (previous spread)
FISH: YELLOW A851 (PA805)   GREENS A544, A251A (PA613, PA694)   BLUE A745 (PA561)   BROWNS A761, A986, A913 (PA474, PA453, PA472)
BACKGROUND: GREY A876 (PA273)
BORDER MOTIF: GREEN A292 (PA603)
BORDER BACKGROUND: GREEN A873 (PA605)

COLOURWAYS FOR OPUS ANGLICANUM (left)
GREEN A874 (PA665)   PINKS A708, A622 (PA846, PA834)
BLUES A883, A886 (PA246, PA564)
COLOURWAYS FOR SERPENT (above)
BLUES A927, A323 (PA570, PA513)   YELLOW A842 (PA734)
RED A503 (PA951)

CHASUBLE REVERSE

This large design is based on an *Opus Anglicanum* chasuble of the mid-thirteenth century which is now in the Museé de Cluny in Paris. It was acquired by the museum at the Baudet sale in Dijon in 1870 and is worked in Florentine stitch with cross-stitch being used for the small single squares. A chasuble is the outermost garment worn by priests when celebrating the Eucharist. It derives from a cloak worn when outdoors by both men and women during the late Roman period. My pattern is based on the repeating motif found on the reverse of the chasuble. I have worked it entirely in petit point but much of the design could be worked in Florentine, especially the outline of the large green motif. A combination of Florentine and cross-stitch is also possible. The effect of combining stitches is to give the finished work a more interesting surface texture.

The heritage of Celtic, Anglo-Saxon, Roman, Elizabethan, Georgian and Victorian art in Britain is remarkable in variety, appeal and influence. Those who are gifted with genius, like the sculptor Henry Moore, add to this continuing artistic wealth, and even William Morris in his social and political desire to regain the lost artistic innocence of the fabled artisan could not dissociate himself from these centuries of achievement. When we sit down to embroider a pattern for a cushion or a rug for a child's bedroom, we are not working in some isolated twentieth-century hobby land, disconnected from our past. We may not know or even care about a thousand years and more of artistic tradition behind our simple efforts, but the influence is there. If a brief study of the subject doesn't show you this, then return to your cross-stitch and recall that it is the *same* stitch Egyptian women did in the times of the Pharoahs – a little stitch that mankind has elevated from utility to art. You have in your hand a living inheritance. All too frequently we think that embroidery was the occasional pastime of ladies. This was certainly true of amateur needlewomen in the great English houses and convents in the past. But the bulk of the church embroideries like *Opus Anglicanum* were produced in professional workshops, most of them in London. These were directed by men and the workers, who included both men and women, often served apprenticeships of up to seven years. The majority of the embroidery of this kind in the thirteenth and fourteenth centuries was carried out in silk and silver gilt thread. Pearls and precious stones were incorporated to make the embroidery akin to jewellery and of immense value.

For the English, many of the symbols and motifs of embroidery spring from Christianity. And so it seemed appropriate to close this pattern book about the countryside, which each spring brings us renewal, with the Easter season when we praise new life.

COLOURWAYS FOR CHASUBLE REVERSE (right)
DIAMOND MOTIFS: GREENS A402, A406 (PA602, PA601)
COLOURED STRIPES: YELLOW A692 (PA754) PINK A203 (PA874)
COLOURWAYS FOR CELTIC MOTIF (above)
RED A448 (PA841)   BLUE A853 (PA513)

COLOURWAYS FOR EASTER FLOWERS (overleaf left)
FLOWERS: REDS A752, A621, A622, A623, A626, A504, A759 (PA935, PA835, PA834, PA833, PA831, PA840, PA900) YELLOWS A471, A474 (PA704, PA726) BROWN A124 (PA484)
LEAVES AND STEMS: GREENS A352, A402, A406 (PA604, PA602, PA601)
ANGEL: GREYS A989, A962, A963 (PA236, PA203, PA202)
CROSS: YELLOWS A471, A474 (PA704, PA726) WHITE A992 (PA261) BROWNS A121, A124 (PA486, PA484)

COLOURWAYS FOR LITTLE FLOWERS (overleaf, above left and right)
FLOWERS: REDS A759, A504, A754, A752 (PA900, PA840, PA934, PA935) YELLOW A474 (PA726)
LEAVES AND STEMS: GREENS A352, A402, A406 (PA604, PA602, PA601)

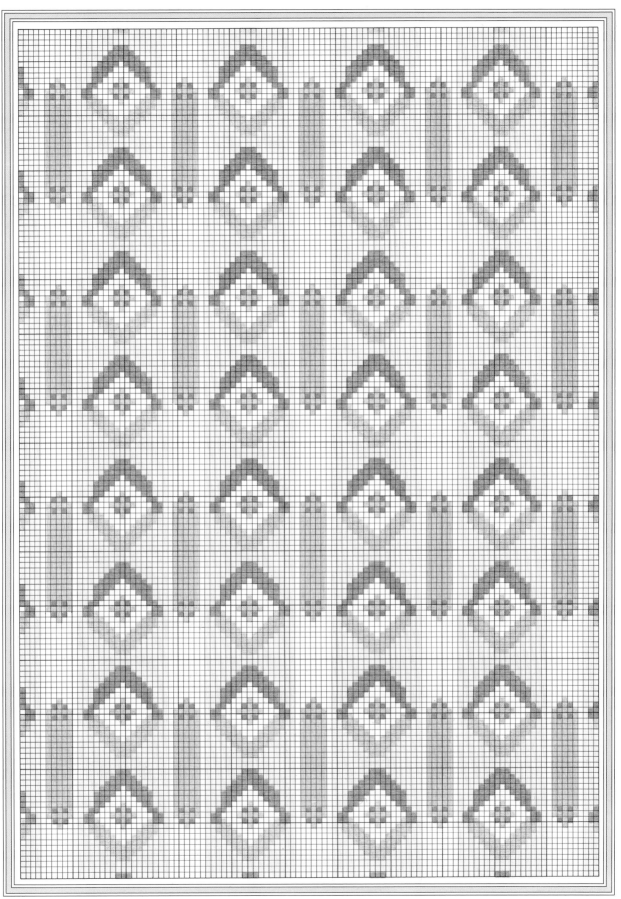

EASTER FLOWERS

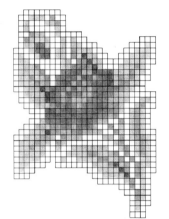

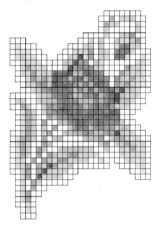

Praise the Lord from the heavens,
praise him in the heights.
Praise him, all his angels,
praise him, all his host.

Praise him, sun and moon,
praise him, shining stars.
Praise him, highest heavens
and the waters above the heavens.

Let them praise the name of the Lord.
He commanded: they were made.
He fixed them for ever,
gave a law which shall not pass away.

Praise the Lord from the earth,
sea creatures and all oceans,
fire and hail, snow and mist,
stormy winds that obey his word;

all mountains and hills,
all fruit trees and cedars,
beasts, wild and tame,
reptiles and birds on the wing;

all earth's kings and peoples,
earth's princes and rulers;
young men and maidens,
old men together with children.

Let them praise the name of the Lord
for he alone is exalted.
The splendour of his name
reaches beyond heaven and earth.

Psalm 148

ACKNOWLEDGEMENTS

I am grateful to Jo Corfield, Sr Paula Dansen OSB, Brendan Clifford and Robert Nightingale for their help, and to the monks of the Monastery of Christ Our Saviour, Turvey, Bedfordshire, for their encouragement and support while I wrote this book.

The publishers would like to thank the Bridgeman Art Library for permission to reproduce the following paintings: *Chickens and Pigeons in an Outhouse*, 1921, by Edgar Hunt (1876-1953), pp. 20-21 (The Eaton Gallery); *Still Life With Strawberries*, by W. Weiss (c. 1840), p. 22 (Roy Miles Fine Art Paintings). The publishers would also like to thank the Fine Art Picture Library Ltd for permission to reproduce the following: *Stolen Cherries*, by Frederick Morgan (1856-1927), p. 6; *A Cornfield, Kent*, by Alfred Augustus Glendening (fl. 1861-1903), pp. 8-9; *The Path by the Water Lane*, by Miles Birket Foster, R.W.S. (1825-1899), p. 10; *Picking Waterlilies from a Punt*, by Frank Percy Wild (1861-1950), pp. 12-13); *Hours of Idleness*, by Sir Luke Fildes, p. 14; *Still Life of Butterflies and Apples*, 1886, by Eloise Harriet Stannard (fl. 1852-1893), p. 15; *Still Life of Plums and a Pear*, by John Sherrin (1819-1896), p. 16); *Spring Flowers*, by Henry James Johnstone (1835-1907), p. 17; *The Haywain*, by Myles Birket Foster (1825-1899); pp. 18-19; *Picking Turnips*, by Robert Cree Crawford (1842-1924), p. 21; *In Love*, by Marcus Stone (1840-1921), p. 35; *The Orchard*, 1901, by William Teulon Blandford Fletcher (1856-1936), p. 36; *Drawing Water by a Cottage*, 1917, by William Kay Blacklock (b. 1872; fl. 1897-1922), p. 42; *Far From the Madding Crowd*, by Henry John Yeend King (1855-1924), p. 86; the Victoria and Albert Museum for *Water Meadows Near Salisbury*, 1829, by John Constable (1776-1837) pp. 24-25; Sue Atkinson for the photographs which appear at the beginning of each chapter: *Flowers and Butterflies cushion*, p. 29 (charted on pp. 66 and 67; *Victorian Roses*, pp. 68-9 (charted on p. 49); *Birds and Flowers*, pp. 88-9 (charted on pp. 94 and 95); *Victorian Jewels, Chasuble Reverse* and *Medlar Tree*, pp. 104-5 (charted on pp. 75, 124 and 119); *Floral Repeat chair and cushion* and *Carved Head*, pp. 114-15 (charted on pp. 62 and 63); and the Brotherhood of Ruralists for *Wild Flowers Still Life*, by Graham Arnold, p. 30. Finally, the publishers would like to thank Graham Nicholson for the hand bound books in the above photographs; Victoria Whiteaker for the watercolour in the Harvest Time photograph on pp. 104-5, and the Picture Frame Workshop, St Leonard's Road, Windsor; Country Style Flowers, Peascod Street, Windsor; Country Furniture, St Leonard's Road, Windsor; O'Connor Brothers, Trinity Yard, St Leonard's Road, Windsor; Woods Garden Centre, Bishop Centre, Taplow, Berks for items lent for these photographs.

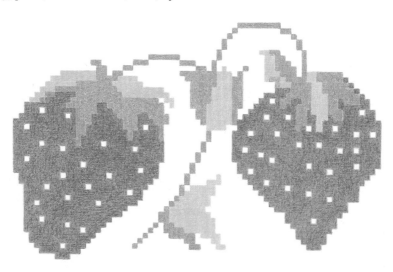